vabnf
781.6409

W9-AEG-180

Less, David A., author
Memphis mayhem
33410016786727   10-22-2020

Memphis Mayhem

DISCARD

Valparaiso Public Library
103 Jefferson Street
Valparaiso, IN 46383

A STORY OF THE MUSIC ★ THAT SHOOK UP THE WORLD

Memphis Mayhem

★ DAVID A. LESS ★

Copyright © David A. Less, 2020

Published by ECW Press
665 Gerrard Street East
Toronto, Ontario, Canada M4M 1Y2
416-694-3348 / info@ecwpress.com

All rights reserved. No part of this publication may be reproduced, stored in a retrieval system, or transmitted in any form by any process — electronic, mechanical, photocopying, recording, or otherwise — without the prior written permission of the copyright owners and ECW Press. The scanning, uploading, and distribution of this book via the internet or via any other means without the permission of the publisher is illegal and punishable by law. Please purchase only authorized electronic editions, and do not participate in or encourage electronic piracy of copyrighted materials. Your support of the author's rights is appreciated.

Editor for the Press: Michael Holmes
Cover design: Ingrid Paulson
Front cover photos:
"Presley, Elvis Aaron" © ullstein bild Dtl. / Getty Images
"Civil Rights March Commemorating King" © Flip Schulke Archives / Getty Images
"BB KING US Blues guitarist at Hammersmith Odeon London April 1980" © Pictorial Press Ltd / Alamy Stock Photo
"Anne Peebles" © Rick Ivy

LIBRARY AND ARCHIVES CANADA CATALOGUING IN PUBLICATION

Title: Memphis mayhem : a story of the music that shook up the world / David A. Less.

Other titles: Story of the music that changed the world

Names: Less, David A., author.

Identifiers: Canadiana (print) 20200233165
Canadiana (ebook) 20200233351

ISBN 978-1-77041-508-9 (softcover)
ISBN 978-1-77305-568-8 (PDF)
ISBN 978-1-77305-567-1 (EPUB)

Subjects: LCSH: Popular music—Tennessee—Memphis—History and criticism. | LCSH: Popular music—Social aspects—Tennessee—Memphis—History. | LCSH: Music trade—Tennessee—Memphis—History.

Classification: LCC ML3477.8.M46 L47 2020
DDC 781.6409768/19—dc23

PRINTED AND BOUND IN CANADA

PRINTING: MARQUIS   5   4   3   2   1

FOR ANGELA AND EMMA

★

DOT, LEON, AND THE BOYS

★

BILLY JO AND BREWER

CONTENTS

FOREWORD

BY PETER GURALNICK

I wasn't a stranger to Memphis when I met David Less.

I wasn't even entirely a stranger to David Less.

I'm not quite sure how or when we first met, but he was there to greet me when I returned to Memphis in 1980 to begin work on *Sweet Soul Music*—and he has been there ever since. A tireless researcher, a valued colleague, the kind of friend you can always count on if you need any help, but don't worry, it's not all that serious; he's just as quick to share a joke.

David knew everybody. I mean, I had other indispensable guides— I'm not going to name them here; they're all acknowledged in my book. But David was a stalwart from the start, as he would continue to be throughout the years. When the Smithsonian embarked upon what turned into the Rock 'n' Soul project (ultimately, it became a museum in Memphis rather than the exhibit in Washington, DC, it was originally intended to be), it was David who proved to be the link to the community, not just because of all the contacts he had made over the years but because of his deep-seated and empathetic feeling for both the music and the people. We collaborated happily on some of the early interviews. I don't know if you've ever worked with anyone interviewing a subject who is not necessarily presold on the process, but believe me, it isn't easy—in fact, it's a lot easier for the two interviewers to step all over each other's feet. With David, it was always a joy. He was always there as a backup; he took the lead when necessary (which was often); he could be voluble; and he could be quiet—whatever the situation called for, he was never anything less than a steady, guiding hand.

But I haven't even mentioned the comprehensive body of work he has put together on his own over the years, the scrupulously informed, modestly foundational, wide-ranging, and insightful interviews that form the basis for this book. Who else but David would recognize the integral importance of Fred Hutchins, Dub Jenkins, Thomas Pinkston, and Sunbeam Mitchell to telling the story of Memphis, not to mention Harmonica Frank's celebrated fish fries in David's own backyard.

Everyone who has written about Memphis music in recent years has drawn on David's interviews, sometimes with suitable acknowledgment, other times not. I've always cherished the hope that the interviews themselves might be published someday as a kind of oral history of Memphis. But with *Memphis Mayhem* David has delivered something even better, he has created his own warm, anecdotal history of Memphis, enlivened by a relaxed and rambling narrative style perfectly suited to its subject (remember, in Memphis, the singer always lags behind the beat), and a Memphis-centric relish for contradiction, digression, and the unpredictable oddities and quiddities of human behavior—but most of all, the book is marked by a feeling for time and place, and the people that occupied it, in a world that David Less has known so long and so well but that, like any true explorer, he is still discovering.

INTRODUCTION

In its coverage of the assassination of the Reverend Dr. Martin Luther King Jr. in 1968, *Time* magazine called Memphis "a decaying Mississippi river town." True, the city was not then what it had been fifty years before, when William Christopher "W.C." Handy began to notate the blues, but *decaying*? Some Memphians took more umbrage over this description of their hometown than the fact that the civil rights leader of a generation had just been murdered in their backyard.

Memphis had a deserved reputation as a racist city, but it is also a place where black and white musicians traditionally made music together, both onstage and in recording studios. The home to murderers and thieves, artists and entrepreneurs, old money and extreme poverty, Memphis gave birth to music that changed the world. Memphis's tourism site promotes the city as the "Home of Blues, Soul & Rock 'n' Roll." To musicians and music lovers worldwide, it is the cradle of American music.

If we imagine history as like a river, most actions by our planet's billions of inhabitants are only pebbles in the river, affecting only an individual's history. But when an event changes the history of humanity in a profound manner, it makes the river curve and bend. And that's what happened in Memphis: three times the course of history looped through the city to leave a lasting impression. In this place, long charged with interracial tensions, if not outright conflict, each of these events opened a door to bridging the divide between black and white America. In each case, once the door opened, it could never be closed again.

During the first decade of the twentieth century, local musician and composer W.C. Handy notated an African American music he had heard traveling throughout the South. In 1909, he wrote a campaign song based on that music, which he later published as "The Memphis Blues." Then in 1917, Handy introduced the rest of the world to the blues with the publication of the sheet music for his "Beale Street Blues." Keep in mind that before the gramophone popularized recorded music around the time of World War I, printed sheet music was the farthest-reaching means of distributing songs. "Beale Street Blues" also gained wide popularity through its inclusion in the Broadway musical revue *Shubert Gaieties of 1919*.

As a direct result of W.C. Handy's work, this regionally rooted, Memphis-distilled musical form was disseminated internationally and became the bedrock of contemporary popular music.

The second event that profoundly altered history also involved music. On a hot July evening in 1954 in a small, crowded recording studio, producer Sam Phillips and a teenaged Elvis Presley recorded songs that changed the world. Ethnomusicologists may debate whether the first rock and roll recording was "Rocket 88" by Jackie Brenston and His Delta Cats or Elvis's "That's All Right," but most agree it happened in Sam Phillips's studio in Memphis.

Some people said Elvis "stole" black music. I feel that the music was there for the taking. He heard it on the radio and possibly in clubs or on the streets. While he didn't learn it in the same way that contemporary African American musicians did (school, families, parties), his feeling for the music justifies the performance. No one claims British musicians in the 1950s and 1960s stole American music when they commandeered it. Similarly, Elvis seized black music and mutated it into rock and roll.

In the same way that W.C. Handy did not invent the blues, it is inconsequential whether these early Elvis sessions were the first rock and roll records. What is indisputable is their impact. According to Memphis rocker Larry Raspberry, who sang the indelible 1965 hit "Keep On Dancing" with his band, The Gentrys, Elvis was "the tributary of black music into white households."[1]

What followed from Elvis included a youth revolution that improved or at least changed race relations in America and ultimately produced a social shift more inclusive of young people and minorities. Coincidentally, the U.S. Supreme Court's *Brown v. Board of Education of Topeka* decision, requiring public schools to integrate, was adjudicated the same year as Elvis's first recording.

Changes toward equality and civil rights along with the rise to dominance of influence in popular culture of the young may have ultimately happened without Elvis Presley. The dissemination of the blues may have happened without the work of W.C. Handy. But both these men and their activities were primary catalysts for musical, cultural, and social change. The fact that both lived in Memphis, a small Southern city, is something more than coincidence.

The third historically defining moment involving Memphis was the tragedy that brought to a climax our nation's long mistreatment and oppression of African Americans. When the Reverend Dr. Martin Luther King Jr. was shot dead by a sniper on April 4, 1968, while standing on the balcony of the Lorraine Motel, the violence and injustice of racial bigotry entered the homes of establishment America and the rest of the world in an undeniable manner.

A change had been coming. Dr. King's death magnified the inevitability and righteousness of it. His murder forced the United States to face the challenges confronting black Americans in their slow, arduous climb toward equality of rights and opportunities.

Ironically, Dr. King's death also signaled a divide in the city's music community that took years to overcome. Traditionally, legal segregation, church, schools, and social standing separated the races, but music had been the common ground for performers and audiences. After Dr. King was killed in Memphis, the long-standing professional and friendly relationships between musicians of different races suffered a rift that took years to heal.

Beginning in 1962 as the house rhythm section for Stax Records, Booker T. & the M.G.s played on a wide swath of the classic soul music that was recorded in Memphis. When they became a racially mixed group, with two black and two white members, in 1965, the M.G.s epitomized the delicate balance between the races that shaped Memphis music.

In my 1999 interview with Booker T. & the M.G.s' guitarist Steve Cropper, he talked about the King assassination. "I'm not sure Memphis will ever recover from that tragedy," he shared. "I can tell you that prior to that, as far as I know, there was never ever a problem with any color that came through the doors at Stax. Didn't happen. And after that, it was never the same."[2]

That same year, I also spoke with noted session keyboardist Marvell Thomas, who performed with Isaac Hayes and The Temptations and was a member of a prominent black family of Memphis musicians. He is featured on many Stax recordings in the 1960s and 1970s. His father, Rufus Thomas, had the first successful releases for both Sun and Stax Records. His sister Carla Thomas was a major recording star as a teenager in the 1960s, and another sister, Vaneese Thomas, is an in-demand singer, producer, and session vocalist. We sat in the historic Sam C. Phillips Recording Studio where Marvell was very candid about race relations in Memphis.

"You know, it was never a problem," he told me. "The problem, when it arose, was political because of the death of Martin Luther King. And for obvious reasons, although I think they're kind of stupid, people who had grown to trust each other and like each other over many years of working together suddenly became suspicious of each other because of that instance."[3]

The great paradox of Memphis music is that it transcends race and genre while simultaneously being defined by both. It is often the result of racial collaboration but has its genesis in the collision of the races. Blacks and whites in Memphis have an interdependent relationship that dates from the yellow fever epidemics of the 1870s. Except for a short time following the assassination of Dr. King, harmony existed among Memphis musicians regardless of race.

I am about to tell a story of Memphis music. It is a story of a city and a culture that fosters independent thinking in the midst of a strict, conservative society. There is a spirit of self-reliance in Memphis. It is born of the poverty and oppression shared by blacks and whites here, who have nothing to lose and everything to gain.

This is not the ultimate, comprehensive story of Memphis music. I have tried to set the scene for the events, personalities, and circumstances that led to Memphis's rightful recognition as a key capital on the map of American music. I hope it shows the cultural and sociological circumstances in which musicians dwelled as they developed their crafts. I also hope that it highlights the unique environment that nurtured and allowed those musicians to influence world culture in an unusual, perhaps disproportionate manner.

My planning for this story began in the mid-1970s when I received a Younger Scholars grant from the National Endowment for the Humanities to study urban music in Memphis. Research continued from that point accelerating in 1990 when the Smithsonian Institution hired me to schedule and conduct interviews as part of the team developing what became the Memphis Rock 'n' Soul Museum. This book draws on over forty years of research including those interviews.

Many notable artists, especially more contemporary ones, are either not mentioned in this book or given short shrift. To those deserving singers, songwriters, musicians, and promoters, I apologize. Any omission is indicative of my particular perspective in telling this story and not the value of their contributions.

CHAPTER ONE

MUTUAL ADMIRATION

"And somebody said, 'That's John Lennon.' So, I just laughed."
—Ann Peebles, soul singer

★

A story circulated among Memphis musicians a few years ago about Blair Cunningham, a member of a legendary family of local drummers, who had moved to England to pursue his career. Cunningham's older brother Carl was a member of the original Bar-Kays and was killed in the airplane crash that claimed most of his bandmates and soul singer Otis Redding.

According to the story, in the early 1990s, Blair was invited to try out for a new band being formed by Paul McCartney. He dutifully went to the former Beatle's estate where he and Paul jammed alone together for a few hours, McCartney on guitar and Cunningham on drums.

At the end of the session, the young drummer from Memphis told the bassist of the most successful rock band in history that they might have a good band if they could find a good bass player.

Cunningham got the job and played with McCartney for a few years. The point of the story is not to disparage him for not knowing McCartney's background. He came from a family of musicians and certainly knew The Beatles' music. But musicians in Memphis were often enveloped in a cocoon of the region's great music.

It was less important to those artists what other people were doing. What was being created in Memphis was what mattered . . .

★

Growing up in Memphis in the 1950s and 1960s, I was unaware of any national significance of local racial, musical, or political issues. We were such a provincial city that it seemed unlikely that anything occurring here impacted the conversation in larger markets. The country was facing major changes in light of newly passed civil rights laws. The onslaught of mass media was making the world seem smaller, even if the South tried to hold on to its distinct regional culture.

The expansion of national chains like McDonald's, Kentucky Fried Chicken, and Memphis-born Holiday Inn promised to erase any semblance of local flair to their products. Patrons were assured the same experience at these establishments regardless of geography. And kids nationwide were all hearing and dancing to the same music thanks to Dick Clark's *American Bandstand*. When Ed Sullivan first introduced Elvis Presley on September 9, 1956, and The Beatles on February 9, 1964, to prime-time TV, the entire country took notice.

Like many others, my family moved to the economically segregated suburbs when faced with the prospect of integrated neighborhoods. My childhood mirrored those of thousands of white kids across the country. The distinction was in the music that came from my hometown.

By the time I entered junior high school in September 1964, the question was not "Do you play an instrument?" but rather "What instrument do you play?" Certainly, part of this evolution of musicians was due to the influence of The Beatles. In fact, I began playing drums because of Ringo Starr.

But there is a long Memphis tradition of children learning an instrument that precedes the British Invasion. It's part of the culture. And in our bands in the 1960s, we played what we knew, which included what we heard from other local bands and popular music from the radio. At our proms and dances, we heard legendary African American bandleaders like Willie Mitchell and Gene "Bowlegs" Miller. On the radio, we listened to Rufus Thomas on WDIA, the first all-black station in the United States.

As a teenager in Memphis, I assumed that there was an Elvis Presley living in every town. Or that some version of Charlie Rich or Ronnie Milsap played piano at local night spots. If you had a decent high school band like The Gentrys or The Box Tops, you could make a hit record at Chips Moman's American Sound Studio. Stax Records was our record label, and its stars were seen around town at the grocery stores or the Poplar Tunes record shop. Booker T. & the M.G.s did a free show at the Overton Park Shell, where the Memphis Country Blues Festival was held annually and featured regional elder blues legends like Furry Lewis, Gus Cannon, Bukka White, and others.

Until I first moved away for college in 1970, I had no idea that there was anything different about Memphis.

★

It was 1967 and popular music was in transition. Successful British newcomers The Who and U.S. expatriate Jimi Hendrix were bridging the divide and bringing their music to the States. Established English performers The Beatles and The Rolling Stones were expanding musical boundaries with *Sgt. Pepper's Lonely Hearts Club Band* and *Their Satanic Majesties Request*, respectively.

Meanwhile, the mainstays at Stax Records in Memphis really didn't have a sense of how far their music was reaching outside of their hometown. Otis Redding had visited the United Kingdom for a short tour in 1966, but the label's owner, Jim Stewart, was reluctant to have his house band, Booker T. & the M.G.s, out of the studio for too long. The quartet played on most of the records made at the tiny studio in Memphis, and Stewart didn't want to shut down production for an extended period of time.

Stax vice president Al Bell felt there was an opportunity to increase overseas sales and favored the idea. Finally, Stewart planned a thirteen-show European tour beginning March 17 and running until April 9, 1967. The revue featured the label's most popular acts anchored by Redding. The lineup also included Carla Thomas, The Mar-Keys, Sam & Dave, Eddie Floyd, and Arthur Conley. Booker T. & the M.G.s backed all the singers, and the horn section from The

Mar-Keys joined them to form the house band. Most of the participants were in their twenties and completely unaware of the worldwide following for their music.

According to The Mar-Keys' trumpeter Wayne Jackson, "We didn't have any idea that we were making any impact except the songs were going up and down the charts."[1]

"The Stax/Volt Tour of 1967 was the first time we got a chance to go overseas. The Big Stax Show on the Road," said saxophonist Andrew Love. "When we landed in England, we had limos provided by The Beatles. That's when we began to think, 'Hey, maybe we're somebody.'"[2]

Before the revue tour began, Carla Thomas played with Booker T. & the M.G.s at a small club in London called Bag O'Nails. Beatle Paul McCartney showed up. Years later, she reminisced, "It was to get the practice and it was a real intimate little place. Of course, that just made us feel really good that he came to see us. . . . And we all sat at the table and talked to him and he stayed the whole night, just until about the club closed. He was in awe. He was wonderful. It was just an exchange of mutual admiration."[3]

★

"I love you!" yelled the man in the audience.

The diminutive soul singer with the big voice ignored the outburst. She was accustomed to rowdy admirers. After all, she had played in the clubs in Memphis. And this was the legendary Troubadour, one of the top showcase clubs in Los Angeles. She had dealt with hecklers before. What could go wrong?

"I love you!" shouted the obviously intoxicated man again.

This was Memphian Ann Peebles's big showcase. The Troubadour was *the* hot club in town where stars and music aficionados gathered. Where careers could be launched and the elusive "buzz" could begin.

Decades later, she told me in an interview, "I looked out in the audience and somebody just kept screaming my name and screaming, 'I love you. I love you.' And I kept looking and I was saying, 'Who is this?' I kept looking out and I saw him, but he had a sanitary napkin taped to his

RICK IVY

Ann Peebles at Royal Studios, Memphis

forehead. And he kept screaming and screaming. I said, 'Who is that?' And somebody said, 'That's John Lennon.' So, I just laughed."[4]

It was 1974 and Lennon had moved to Los Angeles and begun an eighteen-month period of debauchery. He had gone to the Troubadour with friends to listen to Peebles. Her rendition of "I Can't Stand the Rain" had been released a year earlier, and Lennon had declared it to be "the best song ever" in *Billboard* magazine. That evening, he was inebriated and had slipped into the ladies' room, emerging with a sanitary napkin across his forehead. As the evening wore on, his declarations of admiration for the soul singer from Memphis grew more graphic. After the show, he came backstage and apologized to Peebles.

"He came backstage and we had a long talk. He's a funny guy."[5]

★

Twentieth-century music is a difficult art form to force into genres. Lines blur between blues, jazz, rock and roll, and R&B. Many of these terms are primarily marketing tools to help retailers and radio stations target consumers.

Congress designated Memphis the "Home of the Blues" on December 15, 1977, probably because of the sheet music and early recordings of band leader W.C. Handy, whose contributions cannot be discounted. Likewise, New Orleans lays claim to its place as the birthplace of jazz based on descriptions of the music played by early pioneer Buddy Bolden, whose renditions were not recorded. The reports of improvisation in his performances are a powerful harbinger of jazz.

Truthfully, both cities' claims are probably not accurate as the instrumentation and repertoire seemed similar between Handy's and Bolden's bands. In fact, music can seldom point to a singular event as its genesis. Even Elvis Presley's first rock recordings stemmed from his love of R&B.

Handy's band read music and played a stricter, more formal style than Bolden's, but musicians and the black audiences likely traveled frequently between the two cities. Both are on the Mississippi River and offered jobs, entertainment, and a population that included the first generation of African Americans born after slavery was abolished.

As American music developed, pockets of innovation existed in many U.S. cities, including clubs on Elm Street in Dallas and those on Decatur Street in Atlanta. But regional differences were often pronounced and led to distinct characteristics that shaped the progression of the music. Such was the case in Memphis.

What is it about this small Southern town that produced music that so enthralled the most famous musicians in the world? Why would both Paul McCartney and John Lennon, the most successful songwriters and musicians of that era, act like fawning fans of its artists?

It's all part of the story of the music from Memphis.

CHAPTER TWO

RACE RELATIONS

"Mrs. Moss, she went to jail,
Called on Judge Dubose,
Judge Dubose came out and said,
'Get right on away from here.'"
—Local song from 1892

★

The city of Memphis never had an exclusive on racism, despite its history as a major slave-trading center. After all, enslaved people were sold and traded as property in many states in the South. But because of these historical atrocities committed by whites upon slaves, Southern whites and blacks have a different relationship than those who live elsewhere in the country.

Marvell Thomas, Memphis musical family scion, said that the major difference between racism in the South as opposed to the North is that racism here has always been overt. Everybody knew where everybody stood on the subject.

Historically, Southern whites and Southern blacks all grew up in an agrarian society. They knew each other because they worked in close contact with each other all the time. The kids grew up playing with each other on the farms and in the streets until they were teenagers. In the segregated North, there was less personal, social contact.

As a river port, Memphis imported diverse regional influences and exported its innovations. Coupled with the ratio of blacks unable to leave Memphis to whites returning after the yellow fever epidemics in the 1870s, the dynamics were set for the intersection of African American and European American music and culture.

There is a misconception that African American music is African music played by black Americans. While many of the instruments and techniques of African American music have a direct link to Africa, the music itself emerged from age-old African and European traditions as they endured in the United States. The banjo, fiddle, and the diddley bow can all be traced to Africa, while the saxophone, guitar, and the diatonic scale were European inventions. The diatonic scale, the basis for Western music, includes a mix of whole and half steps, which music students learn as do, re, mi, fa, so, la, ti, do.

African American music has antecedents retained from slave music (talking drums, work songs, and chants), but as instruments were introduced after slavery was abolished, the music changed. In the South, the people freed from slavery introduced their African heritages to European-trained musicians and, conversely, learned European-devised musical concepts. Strangely enough, it was the racial imbalance in the relationship between black and white Memphians that allowed the music to evolve in a unique fashion.

The story of music in Memphis is full of intersecting moments and the subsequent developments. There are heroes and bystanders, villains and victims, country bumpkins and slick confidence men in a cast of characters that defines the independent spirit.

★

Memphis, founded in 1819 and incorporated in 1826 with a population of 500, was poised to become a major Southern metropolis. Named after the capital of ancient Egypt on the Nile River and situated on a bluff of the Mississippi River, the city grew rapidly over its first five decades until a series of yellow fever epidemics in the 1870s changed its trajectory.

In 1850, black people were 28 percent of Memphis's total population of 8,841. By 1870, the population reached 40,226. However, following a yellow fever epidemic in 1873, the population had grown by only four people over five years. When the worst of the yellow fever epidemics hit Memphis in August 1878, the population shift began. In September of that year, 25,000 people fled the city, leaving fewer than 20,000 in Memphis. Of those who remained, 70 percent were black. Of the Memphians who stayed, one-fourth died.

In 1879, the city of Memphis lost its charter and went bankrupt. The state governed Memphis as a taxing district until 1893 when the charter was restored. By 1880, the population had recovered to 30,000. Freed slaves and other disenfranchised African Americans lived alongside the white Memphians who returned home following the end of the yellow fever epidemics. It was a unique environment that resulted in a synergistic relationship between black and white residents.

In 1865, Congress passed the Thirteenth Amendment formally abolishing slavery. Then on July 28, 1866, the Fourteenth Amendment guaranteed citizenship and equal protection under the law regardless of race. The Fifteenth Amendment gave black men the right to vote when it was ratified on February 3, 1870. Resistance from whites to these laws was strong in Southern former slave-holding states. But Memphis was uniquely positioned because of the racial imbalance created by whites fleeing the city from the epidemics.

As the son of a former slave and a white steamship owner, Robert Church invested in Memphis real estate after the epidemics and amassed a great fortune. Said to be the South's first black millionaire, he was influential in local and national politics during the last decades of the nineteenth century until his death in 1912. Church and his political allies controlled voting blocs by paying poll taxes designed to prevent black men from voting, despite the rights granted by the Fifteenth Amendment.

The combination of Church's influence and their newly granted rights allowed black Memphians to participate in the political process and even hold elected office. From the end of the 1860s until 1890, African Americans served as city councilmen, school board members, county registrar, Shelby County commissioner, and circuit court clerk.

The last elected black in the nineteenth century was Lymus Wallace, who served on the Board of Public Works from 1882 until 1890.

But as more and more white Memphians returned to the city in the early 1890s, black influence waned and tensions between the races intensified.

★

I received a copy of Fred Hutchins's book *What Happened in Memphis* from a friend in 1978. As a twenty-six-year-old graduate student studying Memphis music, my interest was piqued by some of the stories and dry factual information he included.

To my surprise, Hutchins was still listed in the telephone book and answered when I called. He had come to Memphis in 1892 as a four-year-old boy, which made him ninety when we spoke in 1978. He agreed to an interview, and a date was set for my photographer and me to meet him at his home at 1087 Mississippi Boulevard. It was a section of town that had decayed over many years, but Hutchins's home was well-kept and beautiful. The reddish quarry stone house seemed out of place with the more modest ones on the block.

Hutchins was a retired postal worker with a remarkable memory. Coupled with his age, he was able to provide me with facts and stories that may have otherwise been lost to history. He was a slight, light-skinned African American who looked almost like a caricature of himself.

Much like the title character in the Woody Allen film *Zelig*, Hutchins was around greatness but usually in the background. He took violin lessons from Jim Turner, the man who brought W.C. Handy to Memphis. An acquaintance of Handy, he later interviewed the widow of Sim Webb, the fireman with Casey Jones on the legendary train crash near Vaughan, Mississippi, on his ride from Memphis. Webb survived because Jones ordered him to jump before the train crashed.

Fred Hutchins was a bridge between late nineteenth-century and twentieth-century music. As an amatuer musician in Memphis before Handy notated the blues, he spoke of a time when urban black music leaned more on European traditions than African.

Fred Hutchins playing his violin at his home, December 27, 1978

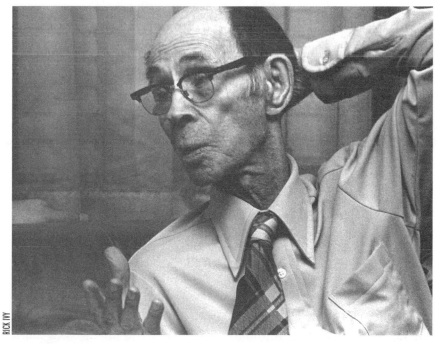

Fred Hutchins reflects on his long life

★

In 1889, eleven prominent black men founded the People's Grocery just outside the Memphis city limits in the "Curve," where the railed streetcars curved off Mississippi Street onto Walker Avenue. They settled on a location on the southeast corner of Mississippi Boulevard and Walker. Across the street on the southwest corner was a grocery owned by a white man named William Barrett.

A few years later, the managing trio of partners of the People's Grocery began advertising lower prices and attracting white patrons in addition to their core black clientele. In the transitional days between the long cold winter and spring, hard feelings exploded into violence.

Trouble began innocently enough on Wednesday, March 2, 1892. Two boys, Armour Harris and Cornelius Hurst, argued over a game of marbles just outside the People's Grocery. Cornelius was white, and when his father began beating Armour, who was black, the store's partners William Stewart and Calvin McDowell interceded. The fight escalated as black and white onlookers joined the fray.

Barrett, owner of the white grocery, was struck and identified Stewart as his assailant. He returned the next day with a police officer. When Calvin McDowell told them that no one matching Stewart's description was in the store, a furious Barrett hit him with his pistol and then dropped it. McDowell grabbed the pistol and shot at Barrett, missing him. Calvin was arrested and released on bond the next day, which was Friday.

That Saturday, Judge Julius Dubose, a former Confederate soldier, declared People's Grocery a public nuisance and vowed to form a posse to get the troublemakers.

Fearing for their safety, Stewart, McDowell, and their partner Thomas Moss consulted an attorney who told them not to count on police protection since they were outside the city limits. He advised them to prepare to defend themselves.

That evening, six white men, including a county sheriff and five deputized civilians, surrounded the People's Grocery to arrest William Stewart for the alleged attack on Barrett a few days earlier. Terrorized black employees and patrons braced themselves for trouble when they realized that they were surrounded.

Gunfire ensued as the sheriff and deputies entered the store. Deputy Charley Cole was shot in the face, and one other lawman was wounded. Retreating to Barrett's store across the street, several more white men were deputized and the skirmish continued. Eventually, thirteen African Americans, including McDowell and Stewart, were arrested, with their weapons and ammunition confiscated.

Purportedly, when officers of the law had identified themselves, the black men threw down their weapons and surrendered. Thomas Moss had been in the back of the grocery working on the books but left when he heard the gunfire.

On Sunday, hundreds of deputized white men were sent to the Curve to arrest those implicated by the lawmen. Forty African Americans were arrested, including young Armour Harris, whose game of marbles began the trouble, and his mother. As the news spread of the arrests, white men surrounded the jail and members of the all-black Tennessee Rifles group gathered to dissuade a possible lynching.

Moss and his pregnant wife could not have known who would be knocking at the door on that Sunday afternoon. When the deputies arrested Moss, his wife, Betty, told them that Thomas had been at home with her the evening of the shootings. He was arrested and taken to jail despite Mrs. Moss's insistence.

Betty Moss appeared before Judge Dubose on Monday to plead for her husband's release and was told to come back three days later.

But in three days, Thomas was dead.

Tuesday, March 8, 1892, brought the good news that Deputy Cole and the other wounded lawmen would survive, and tensions eased at the Shelby County Jail. The Tennessee Rifles went home to their families comfortable that normalcy would soon return.

By evening, only McDowell, Stewart, and Moss, the alleged ring-leaders of the insurrection, were still detained. The black community felt that those still incarcerated would be safe since the jailhouse was a virtual fortress, impossible to escape from and, more importantly, impossible to break into.

Fred Hutchins wrote about that night in his book. The watchman on duty was a Mr. O'Donnell, who later recounted what happened during his shift: "At two o'clock this morning, I was sitting in the office of the jail with Mr. Seats. I heard a ring at the gate and went to the door of the jail asking who was there."

"Hugh Williams of Whitehaven," came the reply. "I have a prisoner."

"All right. This is the place."

O'Donnell hurried to the gate and unlocked it. Two masked men pushed their way in, but when the jailer asked which man was the prisoner, he realized that he had been duped. Reaching for his pistol, he was restrained.

"We want the keys to the cells where the Negroes are," the two men said.

After tying the night watchman's arms, they let in a small group of white men and delivered McDowell, Stewart, and Moss to the mob of more than seventy-five white men outside. The grocers were then taken from the jail to the Chesapeake and Ohio Railway yard. The white newspaper's detailed description of what followed indicates that reporters may have been tipped off in advance to the planned violence.[1]

Calvin McDowell struggled with his captors and managed to grab a shotgun but was quickly subdued. His hands and fingers were shot and mangled before he received four fatal gunshot wounds to the face.

The mob then turned its attention to William Stewart, who was blasted on the right side of his neck by a shotgun. Described as stoic to the end, he next was shot in the neck and left eye with a pistol.

Thomas Moss was the last to die. Shot in the neck, with his dying words he told his people to go west because there was no justice in Memphis for them.

The *Appeal-Avalanche* ran the story in these few words: "Seventy-five men made an assault on the jail at 2:30 this morning and took three men out. What has become of these three men is known only to the seventy-five men who took them out, but it is a reasonable inference that Judge Lynch has passed sentence on them and the sentence has been executed."[2]

On the afternoon following the murders, rumors circulated that the black community was planning retaliation. Judge Dubose ordered the sheriff to arm a hundred men and to shoot any black person who appeared to be making trouble. The men were sent to confiscate the weapons of the Tennessee Rifles.

Sheriff Perkins went to Kupperschmidt's Gun Store to get arms for the posse, and a group of white men flocked to the store to volunteer. The group took the Linden and Magnolia streetcar to the Curve looking to carry out Judge Dubose's orders.

Deputy Sheriff Hugh White reported a mob of blacks headed to the area with revenge in mind. The group of vigilantes found that report untrue, but they began shooting at any congregating group of black people on sight and then looted the People's Grocery. It was later sold at a bargain price to William Barrett.

As a result of the violence, a song began to circulate in the black community in Memphis:

Tom Moss was an innocent man
He was at home in bed
Teacher of a class in Sunday school
Was shot right through the head

Oh, me, oh my, Lord have mercy on me
Oh, me, oh my, Lord have mercy on me

Mrs. Moss, she went to jail
Called on Judge Dubose
Judge Dubose came out and said
Get right on away from here

Oh, me, oh my, Lord have mercy on me
Oh, me, oh my, Lord have mercy on me

They are roaming the streets with their guns
Looking for us to shoot
All we can do is pray to the Lord
There's nothing else to do

Oh, me, oh my, Lord have mercy on me
Oh, me, oh my, Lord have mercy on me[3]

★

The Lorraine Motel was situated on the southern edge of downtown Memphis. It opened in the 1920s under a different name as a white-only establishment. Then in 1945, it became literally a mom-and-pop operation, owned and operated by Walter and Loree Bailey, a black couple, who added more guest rooms and created a safe haven for black visitors to the city. Walter Bailey renamed it the Lorraine Motel in honor of Loree and her favorite song, "Sweet Lorraine."

With its proximity to downtown and Beale Street, it became a popular spot for black businessmen and entertainers who were not allowed in all-white establishments. In the 1960s, it was a favorite hangout for Stax Records artists who were in town recording.

The Baileys welcomed both black and white guests, allowing writers, producers, and Memphis musicians of any race to use the swimming pool, often serving meals poolside. "In the Midnight Hour" and "Knock on Wood," two of the biggest hits on Stax Records, were written at the Lorraine.

Of course, the most famous murder in Memphis occurred there on April 4, 1968. On that day, the Reverend Dr. Martin Luther King Jr. stood on the balcony of the Lorraine Motel, imploring saxophonist Ben Branch to play "Precious Lord" when a shot rang out, ending King's life and putting a permanent stain on Memphis.

In a way, the assassin killed two prominent black people that day. Loree "Sweet Lorraine" Bailey had a stroke when she heard the shot and died five days later.

★

In 1978, ten years after the assassination of Dr. King, race relations were improving but were still fractured. Memphis continued to be a segregated city, despite the 1954 *Brown v. Board of Education of Topeka* decision and the landmark Civil Rights Act of 1964.

As in many communities, Memphis experienced "white flight" to the suburbs in the 1960s and 1970s. In the mid-1960s, the Memphis City Schools district had 130,000 white students. By 1973, the number dwindled to 71,000 white students; four years later, white enrollment was 30,000.

The suburbs were largely white while the inner city was primarily African American. Most white Memphians lived, shopped, and went to school apart from black Memphians. They had little contact with this fast-growing segment of the local population, other than dealing with domestic employees and isolated instances with other workers.

Beale Street, the most famous boulevard in Memphis where W.C. Handy had started his music publishing empire, was already on the National Register of Historic Places. But by the mid-1970s, the entertainment venues that had always dotted Beale had disappeared. Commerce had become limited to Lansky's clothing store, A. Schwab's dry goods store, Art Hutkin's hardware store, and a few pawn shops.

Those pawn shops had lined Beale Street since before the 1970s. Nathan Pritzker was a partner with Nathan Epstein in Nathan's Loans

CARLEEN DORIAN PALMER

Pawn shops on Beale Street, 1970s

at number 178. Epstein's second cousin, Maynard "Sonny" Epstein, had owned Sonny's Loan Office a few doors down at number 166. In 1974, amid the decline of business on Beale Street, Pritzker and the Epsteins joined forces to open a new pawn shop called Nathan and Sonny's Loan Company at 656 Poplar Avenue.

It was a spacious store along one of the major thoroughfares. The city designated an area for pawn shops and this section of Poplar near downtown included several. A plate-glass window in the front was used for display, but all the windows and doors were behind steel mesh for security purposes.

Like many Southern businessmen in their fifties, the three partners were cordial but sometimes patronizing to black people. They had each operated businesses on Beale Street, interacting with their African American employees and customers for three decades. Over the years, they had seen violence toward blacks by both whites and blacks.

Friday, October 6, 1978, began like most days at Nathan and Sonny's Loan Company. They had been in the new location for four years and business was good. Pritzker was not working that day because his wife was a patient at Baptist Memorial Hospital, a short distance away. As usual, the store closed at 5:30 p.m., and Louis Minor, an employee, locked the door at 5:35, leaving the Epstein cousins to count out the day's proceeds.

Sunset was about an hour later, and Nathan Epstein was due at his daughter Judy's home for dinner. When he had not arrived by 7:00 p.m., she called Pritzker to see if her father had stopped at the hospital to visit his partner's wife. Alarmed, Pritzker rushed to the shop to find it ransacked and his partners, Nathan and Sonny Epstein, dead in a back room, each shot in the head.

The door was open, but police deduced that the two men had not been ambushed since their coats and hats were still hung up. There was no sign of a break-in, indicating that they opened the door for the murderer after hours. Police concluded that the killer must have been someone the victims had known.

What initially appeared to be a random robbery proved to be much more. By Saturday, the police had recovered some of the cash and had a suspect in custody. Tony Baldwin, a disgruntled former employee, had been charged two weeks earlier with grand larceny in a complaint filed by Nathan and Sonny's Loan Company over stolen guns. He was charged with the murders.

There had been isolated acts of violence against white Memphians by local African Americans, but Dr. King's assassination had turned already tense race relations even worse. This presumedly calculated murder of prominent white businessmen by a black former employee, which was covered extensively in the daily newspapers and on television, was different. The Epsteins were businessmen who lived in the suburbs, mostly insulated from black people. White Memphians felt their untouchable status had been threatened: if this could happen to the Epstein cousins, it could happen to any white Memphian.

CHAPTER THREE

BLACK NEIGHBORHOOD SCHOOLS

*"When the football teams played, when both schools played,
I wore the pants of one of the schools and the coat of another.
I'd sit on one half with my band and then I'd go over to the
other side for the next."*
— Professor William Theodore McDaniel,
band director at Manassas and Booker T.
Washington High Schools

★

The night after the 1967 class of Memphis's Booker T. Washington High School graduated, a group of neighborhood pals boarded an airplane for New York for the adventure of their lives. Already local celebrities for their hit record "Soul Finger," the Bar-Kays had been hired by their Stax Records label mate Otis Redding for a ten-day stint at the legendary Apollo Theater in Harlem.

Starting the next day, the boys received a rough reception by the boisterous audience in Harlem. These patrons were there to see Otis Redding, one of the hottest stars on the circuit.

"You'd ask the crowd, 'How y'all doing this evening?' No one would respond," said the Bar-Kays' bassist James Alexander. "I can't hear y'all.

How are you doing this evening?' Nobody said nothing. 'Okay, we'd like to do a song for you and we'd like to dedicate it to you.'"[1]

An interracial band, the early Bar-Kays included 1967 Booker T. Washington graduates Jimmie King, Phalon Jones, and Carl Cunningham; a white 1967 Central High School graduate Ronnie Caldwell; 1966 Booker T. Washington graduate Ben Cauley and eleventh grader James Alexander. Except for Caldwell, they all lived in the same neighborhood and had attended the same elementary, middle, and high schools.

The teens played a short opening set and then performed as Redding's backup band. The format for the day's entertainment included a live show followed by a movie. It was typical for an act to perform five shows daily each paired with a movie, often making the workday last twelve hours or more. And when school was out for the summer, parents would drop their children off at the Apollo for the day, knowing they were safe and out of trouble.

The young Bar-Kays only had one uniform each, which they hung up to dry between shows in the dressing room. The boys looked sharp in their shiny maroon polyester suits with pink shirts, silk socks, and black patent leather shoes.

Unfortunately, many in the audience who had been there all day saw them perform in the same clothes for hours.

"So if somebody has been there at a quarter to one and they see us with that same uniform on," explained Alexander with a chuckle. "We might say, 'We're getting ready to play this song for you.' And they'd say, 'Well, when you going to change clothes, because you had that on the last show?'"[2]

The Bar-Kays had been waiting for this moment since April when Redding first hired them as his band. After hearing their performance at the *Goodwill Revue* (an annual charity show produced by Memphis radio station WDIA), he sought them out at the Hippodrome, a club on Beale Street. He had wanted the band to begin touring with him in the spring, but the boys' parents prohibited them from working with him until after graduation in late May.

After the shows in New York, they returned home, occasionally reuniting with Redding over the summer. That September, James Alexander returned to Booker T. Washington for his senior year of high school.

★

The history of teaching music in African American Memphis schools begins in 1927 when a young physical education instructor started a band program at Manassas High School. Twenty-five-year-old Jimmie Lunceford was named Memphis's first band director at a black city school.

Lunceford's student band was called the Chickasaw Syncopators. He merged the high school students with some Nashville musicians he had met at Fisk University, and in 1929, the band was renamed the Jimmie Lunceford Orchestra. The group's popularity grew to rival that of established stars like Count Basie, Fletcher Henderson, and Cab Calloway after they followed the Duke Ellington & His Orchestra's engagement at New York's famed Cotton Club in 1934.

Jimmie Lunceford was the first in a long line of Memphis City Schools' band directors to become a mentor to students in black neighborhoods. The tradition continued until the schools integrated in the 1960s, when kids were sent across town to balance the ratio of black and white students.

While there were many great band directors after the high schools were integrated, students were from a cross section of the city and had not grown up together in the segregated sections of Memphis where their families knew one another as neighbors.

At the same time that Lunceford worked with his band at Manassas, another group of students formed a band at rival Booker T. Washington High School. Led by Dub Jenkins, the young bandmates carved out a reputation as a top dance band in the 1920s.

While the Bar-Kays may have represented the end of that tradition of student bands from segregated neighborhoods, Dub Jenkins and His Playmates were the beginning. Their popularity rivaled the Chickasaw Syncopators and helped establish a friendly competition between the historically black high schools Manassas and Booker T. Washington, later expanding to include the Douglass, Hamilton, and Melrose schools.

"Jimmie Lunceford was the teacher at Manassas High School," said Jenkins, during at interview at his apartment in New York. "And he organized the Chickasaw Syncopators. I was just a student at Booker T.

RICK IVY

RICK IVY

ABOVE: Dub Jenkins at home in New York, March 10, 1979

LEFT: Dub Jenkins relaxing with his saxophone

Washington, and that's where I organized my band called Dub Jenkins and His Playmates."[3]

Jenkins modeled his unit after the popular big bands of the 1920s and 1930s. The Playmates had a brass section with three trumpets and one trombone and a woodwind section with two tenor and two alto saxophones. At times, the alto saxophone players would switch to baritone, an easy change since those two instruments are in the same key, which eliminated the need to learn new scales when adding another instrument. The group was rounded out by a drummer, pianist, and bassist. That was the classic big band format, and it allowed the group to play arrangements of contemporary popular music.

Jenkins's band allegedly gave singer Al Hibbler his first professional job and later featured Dwight "Gatemouth" Moore. As Jenkins's popularity grew in Memphis, he moved to New York, following in the footsteps of Jimmie Lunceford. Unable to replicate Lunceford's success in New York, he gave up music and earned a living as a waiter in Manhattan until his death.

Jimmie Lunceford set the mold for black high school students to study with accomplished band teachers. It became a tradition that continued at Manassas, Booker T. Washington, and later at other black high schools. Based in historically African American neighborhoods, these schools were the centerpieces for social and musical activity.

With limited opportunities for parents to advance in their careers, thereby earning more money, families stayed in the same neighborhoods: children would begin elementary school and continue through high school with essentially the same people. Often beginning band lessons in junior high, they typically practiced and formed bands with their classmates.

Emerson Able, a 1948 Manassas High graduate, reminisced about those days during my interview with him: "What happened in the neighborhood, we would go to someone's house. We would practice together after we left school. Then on Saturdays, the parents would do chili with hot dogs and spaghetti. And it would be nothing for us to go to someone's parents' home and you've got sixteen or seventeen guys in a three-room house, all with instruments playing. The problem was you were ridiculed if you could not play your part. You were put down. I mean peer pressure was a bit much during those days."[4]

★

William Theodore McDaniel began teaching music in the early 1940s at Booker T. Washington. After a year, he was assigned to also teach at Manassas, and he stayed at both high schools as band director until 1948. He continued at Booker T. Washington from 1948 until 1959. Affectionately known as "Professor McDaniel," he worked with the Booker Teasers, the school band at Booker T. Washington, and the Rhythm Bombers, the band at Manassas.

"Whenever Manassas looked good, Booker Washington got mad. Whenever Booker Washington looked good, Manassas got mad. And I was in the middle of it," McDaniel said. "When the football teams played, when both schools played, I wore the pants of one of the schools and the coat of another. I'd sit on one half with my band and then I'd go over to the other side for the next."[5]

The rivalry between the schools in athletics and music motivated students to excel. The competition was so fierce that it was formalized in what they called ballet, an event held annually from at least the 1940s until the schools were integrated in the 1960s.

Floyd Newman, a saxophonist, who was a 1949 graduate of Booker T. Washington, described his high school experience: "During the course of the year, Booker Washington had a thing they called ballet. They would have a big . . . like a Broadway production every year. I mean, just like you would see in New York or something. . . . All the schools would come over, but it was always a battle between the dance band at Booker Washington playing against the dance band at Manassas. It was not only between the two bands, the football team, the basketball teams and everything. That's the way it was, you know. But it was a good rivalry."[6]

The rivalry was still strong when Andrew Love graduated from Booker T. Washington High in 1959. Love was a saxophonist who, as a member of the legendary Memphis Horns, appeared on more than 83 gold and platinum records and fifty-two number-one and 116 top-ten records, including fifteen Grammy winners.

Love recalled, "Manassas and BTW had a big rivalry. We would get down there before the parades and call ourselves cutting heads. See who could play the best, play the most, we'd get tired before the parade started. There would be the battle of the bands, and at the parades, we gathered down to see who would beat each other."[7]

★

Professor McDaniel's term coincided with the advent of an adventurous style of jazz called bebop. Developed in New York City in the 1940s, it became popular among younger listeners who wanted something different than the swing music that had dominated jazz since the 1930s. Professor McDaniel encouraged his students in the Booker Teasers and Rhythm Bombers to play bebop, but he also demanded that they be proficient in reading and playing other kinds of music.

Although Memphis has had a rich jazz scene since the early 1900s, McDaniel's students represented a group of musicians whose influence was recognized internationally. The Memphis jazz scene in the 1940s and early 1950s produced George Coleman, Harold Mabern, Hank Crawford, Charles Lloyd, Booker Little, and Sonny Criss. These artists left Memphis and became legendary as leaders and sidemen. A number of talented jazz musicians from that same period later returned to Memphis, including Fred Ford, Phineas Newborn Jr., his younger brother Calvin Newborn, and Herman Green.

The lineage of top Memphis band directors continued with Emerson Able, Onzie Horne, Andy Goodrich, Floyd Newman, and Matt Garrett who followed Professor McDaniel at Manassas in 1948. The influence of these teachers cannot be understated in the development of Memphis music.

In addition to the great jazz tradition that came from the students of these band directors, these historically black Memphis high schools also count as alumni influential musicians such as Booker T. Jones, keyboardist for Booker T. & the M.G.s; Maurice White, leader of Earth, Wind & Fire; and Isaac Hayes.

★

As graduates in the mid-1960s, the Bar-Kays may have represented the end of a long tradition of Memphis bands forming out of its black schools. Children in African American neighborhoods attended school together from elementary through high school graduation, and when they learned to play music, it was often within this tightly knit community that nurtured them and provided instruction.

This pattern continued until Memphis City Schools adopted the edict of *Brown v. Board of Education of Topeka* and integration became the norm. Although the Supreme Court decision became law in 1954, Memphis schools did not begin to integrate until 1961; the all-white school board constricted the process. Only four black students could enroll into any one school and only one class at a time, beginning with the first grade. The one-grade-at-a-time rule lasted five years. In 1966, the faculty and all grades at all schools were finally integrated.[8]

As more black and white students started attending schools together, school administrators discontinued proms and social events for fear of mixing the races. In 1973, the schools began busing, and the notion of a neighborhood school disappeared. Children from all different parts of the city were students in the same school.

This crucial component of nurturing and developing talent within neighborhoods that was part of the fabric of Memphis music ended with school integration.

Obviously segregated schools were an impediment to equal educational opportunites for African American children. Inadequate funding, facilities, and classrooms contributed to this disparity. Although integrating schools was the only solution, an unfortunate side effect was the loss of neighborhood schools.

CHAPTER FOUR

THE RACIAL BRIDGE

"Rock and roll is part of a plot to undermine the morals of the youth of our nation. It is sexualistic, unmoralistic, and the best way to bring people of both races together."
—Asa Carter, Ku Klux Klan leader and past secretary of the North Alabama Citizens' Council

★

Asa Carter could not have known how prophetic his statement would prove. Music would unite the races in ways politicians and preachers could only imagine.

The 1950s were the salad years for white families in America. Riding the wave of new opportunities brought by the GI Bill after World War II, most citizens were convinced that the United States was better than any other place in the world. And for white America, it probably was.

The threat of Soviet militarism only served to reinforce the solidarity of Americanism and the U.S.'s sense of moral superiority. African Americans were still oppressed, but there were tremors of support foreshadowing the upcoming civil rights movement. In 1954, the Supreme Court's *Brown v. Board of Education* ruling declared state laws that established separate school systems for blacks and whites to be unconstitutional.

There were many signs of change on the horizon. In the early days of television, white people were featured in leading roles while blacks were often cast as their foils (i.e., Rochester on *The Jack Benny Program*). Historically lighter-skinned African Americans were considered more palatable to white sensibilities. When dark-skinned black singer/musician Nat King Cole hosted his television program, *The Nat King Cole Show*, on NBC from November 1956 to December 1957, it featured other popular black performers, including Count Basie, Pearl Bailey, Harry Belafonte, and Sammy Davis Jr. as guests. It initially aired for only fifteen minutes on Mondays from 7:30 to 7:45 p.m. and later expanded to thirty minutes on Tuesdays at 7:30 p.m. and 10:00 p.m., but the program failed to secure steady, national sponsorships and was subsequently canceled.

American Bandstand with host Dick Clark was syndicated through the ABC television network in 1957. Formerly a local broadcast in Philadelphia, *Bandstand* exposed rock and roll and R&B records to a national audience, with Clark introducing bands and singers lip-synching their hits as white teenagers danced to the records in the television studio. In 1964, the on-screen dancers were integrated.

There was an uptick of homogenization in America. Rural and urban audiences saw and heard the same news and entertainment at approximately the same time each day via the three nationwide television networks and their radio subsidiaries. There were still regional distinctions in musical preferences and cultural mores, but the world was about to seem smaller just as the market for music from Memphis was on the verge of exploding.

Certain radio stations allowed free-thinking white disc jockeys to play black music at select hours, usually at night. Some stations had clear-signal radio transmissions, strong enough in the evening when other stations had signed off the air, that penetrated the enclaves of white America in unexpected ways. They brought "race records," songs that were recorded by and marketed to African Americans, to a generation of white teenagers exposed to mass media for the first time through movies, radio, and television.

In 1949, Memphis radio station WDIA converted to an all-black format, the first of its kind in the world by playing race records with African American on-air personalities. That same year on WHBQ, disc jockey Dewey Phillips, aka Daddy-O-Dewey, played an eclectic mix that included race records, thus exposing young white Memphians to black music. Clear channel out-of-town stations like Nashville's WLAC widened the reach of blues and gospel for music-hungry teens, including one named Elvis Presley.

Attitudes were shifting among white American teenagers when nineteen-year-old Presley recorded an Arthur "Big Boy" Crudup blues song "That's All Right" in Sam Phillips's tiny studio in July 1954. He and the band were just goofing around during a break from a recording session when Phillips encouraged them to continue and recorded it. The story has been told many times: Presley's historic rise in popularity shook the foundations of white America by bringing black music into its homes through its children, who followed his rise on records, radio, television, and eventually movies.

In 1955, Bill Haley and His Comets blared "Rock Around the Clock" in the film of that name. On September 9, 1956, Ed Sullivan called Presley "a real decent, fine boy" on his popular Sunday evening television program. As a result, this new music entered the consciousness of conventional America. The genie was let out of the bottle, and rock and roll spread across the world.

As the epicenter of the burst of rock music that began with Presley, Memphis was geographically and culturally positioned to lead the world down the path that Asa Carter, the Ku Klux Klan leader, warned about: "Rock and roll is part of a plot to undermine the morals of the youth of our nation. . . . sexualistic, unmoralistic, and the best way to bring people of both races together."[1] Memphis was primed for the collision course that followed.

★

Situated on the Mississippi River in nearly the center of America, Memphis had long attracted people from a hundred-mile radius to visit, shop, and be entertained. Many people also moved here from the farms in nearby Mississippi and Arkansas for better opportunities, especially in the wake of agricultural industrialization.

But black and white transplants found two different sides of the city.

For whites, Memphis offered jobs, housing, shopping, and entertainment. Blacks found low-paying jobs and housing in segregated neighborhoods. Many blacks continued their migration up river to St. Louis, Chicago, and Detroit, following the promise of better-paying jobs in factories.

The common denominator for both black and white residents of Memphis was entertainment, which was loved by everyone. Music for whites and blacks was everywhere. With its reputation as a wide-open town, Memphis had historically been a center of nightlife for both races, with separate venues and plenty of them.

White Memphians in the 1950s frequented upscale nightclubs that featured music, dinner, and drinks (patrons could bring alcohol and pay for glasses), venues such as the Eagle's Nest, Silver Slipper, Clearpool, and Five Gables — all of which were transitioning from big band to an early style of rock and roll called rockabilly music (a hybrid of R&B and country music). Across the Mississippi River were three clubs that featured black bands and dancing. They could also attend the Thursday Midnight Rambles all-black shows at the Palace Theatre on Beale Street where local artists like B.B. King, Bobby "Blue" Bland, and others competed for prizes.

Black patrons in the 1950s frequented clubs in the African American neighborhoods of Binghampton, New Chicago, and Orange Mound. Clubs in the areas surrounding Beale Street included Clifford Miller's Flamingo Room and Andrew "Sunbeam" Mitchell's Club Handy. The Brown Derby was in Orange Mound and Currie's Club Tropicana was in North Memphis on Wellington.

Many of these venues featured jazz rather than strict blues or R&B, but Memphis musicians at that time played every style to please their audiences. In the after-hours jazz world of Memphis as early as the 1940s, white and black musicians played together in African American clubs.

Mississippi-born white musician Mose Allison claimed to have sneaked into Club Handy on Beale Street in the late 1940s. And there are rumours that Elvis Presley sometime sat in with black bands at the Flamingo Club. Steve Cropper, also white, remembered that, as a teenager in the 1950s, he listened to music emanating from Club Handy.

"We used to go downtown to the Club Handy," Cropper recalled. "And they wouldn't let us in. They knew we were underage, but they would let us stand in the stairwell. You could look past the ticket booth that stood in the way to getting in, and there was a mirror in the back of the club. You could see the reflection of the band in that mirror."[2]

The success of Elvis Presley catapulted record producer Sam Phillips and his Sun Records label to the forefront of the rock revolution. Young aspiring rockers hoping to be the next Presley flocked to Memphis.

The first generation of these white musicians whose music was genuinely influenced by the region's black culture arrived at Sun Studio in the mid-1950s. Among them were Jerry Lee Lewis, Carl Perkins, Johnny Cash, Charlie Rich, Sonny Burgess, Warren Smith, Charlie Feathers, Billy Lee Riley, and later Roy Orbison.

The impact of rockabilly on the world was enormous. The generation of Memphis musicians who were still in high school in the mid-1950s benefited from the continuing melding of styles between first-generation rock and rollers and the local African American music prevalent during that era.

If rockabilly represented a collision of white hillbilly music and black R&B, then the next culture crash was between rockabilly and electric blues. That happened on an international basis as 1950s British teens were inspired by the music of Memphis and Chicago. It manifested in the early 1960s British Invasion of The Beatles, The Rolling Stones, and John Mayall & the Bluesbreakers.

The music was foreign and exotic to teenagers from afar, but it was simply local to those in Memphis. It was folk music in the classic sense—handed down by oral tradition—despite its global reach. White high school students, who heard great black local bands, developed into musicians well-versed in both white rockabilly and black R&B.

★

Steve Cropper, Donald "Duck" Dunn, and Don Nix met in grade school at Sherwood Elementary. They grew up in a world where the dad went to work and the mom stayed home to tend to the house and raise the kids, who were allowed to roam on their bicycles as long as they were home for dinner.

"I met Duck in the fifth grade and Cropper about a year later," Nix said. "We all went to Sherwood school and then we went to Messick High School."[3]

In the Memphis City Schools system, Messick High School was an all-white suburban school, typical of the 1950s. It had school dances, football games, and all the diversions that insulated white teens of working-class families from the unpleasant realities of systemic racism. But despite the marginalization of African Americans on film, print, and early television, this group of white Messick High School students developed a passion that led them to a lifetime of transracial music.

All three were born in 1941 and started high school in 1955, the year Elvis's contract was sold to RCA Records. That label released his first long-playing album, simply titled *Elvis Presley*, in March 1956, catapulting him from a regional sensation to an international star. Meanwhile at Messick, Cropper met other like-minded kids and in the eleventh grade began playing music.

Daddy-O-Dewey Phillips was spreading the gospel of black music on the radio with an eclectic mix of styles and artists that reached impressionable ears, including those of the Messick High School students. Ruben Cherry had a record shop on Beale Street called Home of the Blues, and he played race records for the high school kids who came by on the weekends.

"We were spending our time learning and jamming on guitars, playing with our friend Charlie Freeman," Cropper said. "Charlie was taking lessons from a guy named Lyn Vernon. I used to go over at his house after his lessons and he'd try to teach me what Lyn taught him, and we'd just sit around the house and jam."[4]

These impromptu after-school jam sessions later included fellow Messick students Terry Johnson on drums and Donald "Duck" Dunn on guitar. But Dunn had trouble with the guitar and switched to bass, trading six strings for four.

Cropper explained the band's expansion, "This kid comes up to me one day, says, 'I want to be in your band.'

"I said, 'We're really not looking for anybody. What do you do?'

"'I play saxophone.'

"'I don't think we're going to add horns to the band,' I said. 'You know, two guitars, bass, and drums is what we got. How long have you been playing?'

"'I've been taking lessons for like three months.'

"And I remember like it happened yesterday, he said, 'My uncle and my mother have a recording studio.'

"Hello? And I said, 'Why don't you come by Saturday? We're going to rehearse Saturday morning about ten over at Terry's house. Come by and we'll see what you can do.'

"If he hadn't said he had a recording studio, that would have been the end of that conversation. I don't know what would have happened to Packy Axton. But, man, he turned out to be one of the best saxophone players for soul and feel."[5]

CHAPTER FIVE

THAT WAS JUST MEMPHIS

"We didn't know that everybody didn't play that kind of music. That was just Memphis."
— Don Nix, musician, producer

★

Memphis is situated on the bluff where Spanish explorer Hernando de Soto first crossed the Mississippi River in 1541. Colonizing settlers first filed claims on the land around 1783. In 1819, the city of Memphis was founded by three entrepreneurs: Judge John Overton, James Winchester, and General Andrew Jackson, who became the seventh president of the United States.

In 1830, when Jackson was president, the Indian Removal Act forced thousands of Native Americans from their lands east of the Mississippi. Between 1830 and 1837, 46,000 Native Americans traveled the infamous Trail of Tears, part of which passed through Memphis.

The Great Migration of Southern blacks, who were seeking better employment opportunities and living conditions, from rural areas to points north, which included Memphis, St. Louis, and Chicago, started less than a hundred years later and continued until roughly 1970. Country blacks facing institutional racism and unchecked violence from Southern whites hoped for an improved lifestyle by moving to a big city. That exodus changed the country's demographics. More than 89 percent of African Americans lived in the Southern states in 1910, but by 1970 only 53 percent remained. The period of greatest change occurred from the 1940s to the early 1960s.

At the literal crossroads of these two major migrations, Memphis saw diverse transient populations. Situated in the southwest corner of the state of Tennessee, Memphis is bordered by Mississippi on the south and Arkansas across the Mississippi River on the west. Musicians poured into Memphis from all sides, especially in the 1950s when black music exploded into mainstream popularity.

The 1950s kids liberated by Elvis and the early rockers often got their first taste of live black music in West Memphis, Arkansas, which shares its musical pedigree with Memphis proper. The three most influential nightclubs there were the Cotton Club, Danny's, and the Plantation Inn. The Cotton Club and Danny's were relatively strict about not allowing teenagers entry, but the Plantation Inn was accommodating to underage music aficionados. Despite its lax admission policy for underage patrons, segregation was strictly enforced. It was in a stand-alone building located just on the Arkansas side of the bridge that spans the Mississippi, connecting Memphis and West Memphis. Opened in 1942, the nightclub was owned by Morris and Clemmye Berger and their son, Louis Jack. The Plantation Inn was recognizable by the giant neon sign on its roof featuring a dancing couple over the words "having fun with Morris." It catered to a white audience and usually featured black bands.

On hot days, the doors were propped open with a fan blowing the smoke out, and the sounds of R&B permeated the evening air. During their breaks, the black musicians were not allowed to socialize in the club, so they exited into the parking lot. Music-hungry Memphis teenagers often met the bands in the parking lot, which led to the flourishing of mixed-race friendships in the 1960s.

At Danny's, the entertainment was often either trumpeter Willie Mitchell's band or tenor saxophonist Ben Branch's band, although both groups sometimes performed at the Plantation Inn, too. Branch and Mitchell were important African American musicians whose groups developed local talent for decades.

Mitchell's, Gene "Bowlegs" Miller's, and Branch's bands were also sometimes heard by teenagers on Sundays, when liquor could not be sold or served in West Memphis. Many of the influential black bands played at Catholic Youth Organization (CYO) dances in Memphis. These dances and school proms introduced exceptional black bands to white Memphis youth who did not venture over the bridge to West Memphis.

★

Asa Carter's prediction that music would bring both races together was something most white parents at that time desperately wanted to avoid, making them reluctant to allow their children to explore a new sense of independence characterized by rock and roll. Although white teenagers in mid-1950s Memphis soaked up blues and rock and roll on the radio and from the occasional television or movie appearance, there were only a few parent-approved venues where these teens could hear this music live.

Don Nix described one of these venues and the forbidden allure of black music during that time. I spoke with him at his home outside Nashville. For an artist often referred to as obscure, Nix has been involved in numerous high-profile projects, including producing important records of Albert King, John Mayall, Jeff Beck, Delaney and

Don Nix at Memphis Music Exhibit, Brooks Memorial Art Gallery, September 2, 1976

RICK IVY

Bonnie, and Freddie King. His song "Going Down" has been recorded by a range of artists from Leon Russell to Deep Purple. As a teenager in the 1950s, he grew up during the Eisenhower years of peace and prosperity.

"The only place to go was called the Casino. It was at the Fairgrounds. It was an old ballroom that they tore down later—a huge domed building. The Parks Department made it into a place for teenagers to go on the weekends. You got a card, and as you went in, they would punch the card. You had to be in high school—any school, and there were only eight high schools in Memphis at the time. Everything started there on a Friday night. Everybody would go there."[1]

Leaning back in his chair, Nix grinned as he remembered his early exposure to live music played by an African American band. "At the Casino, I started hearing about this place across the river, this great place for music. So I got a ride over there one night, and of course from then on, it was every weekend we'd go over there. It was Sissy Charles [Charles "Tennessee" Turner] and his band, and this guy was great. He was openly gay. He would peroxide his hair blond, had real long hair.

"There was no other band in the world like that band and we were getting to hear it. We didn't know that everybody didn't play that kind of music. That was just Memphis."[2]

★

As the bassist for Booker T. & the M.G.s, Donald "Duck" Dunn is considered a pioneer of soul music. Although mixed-race jazz jam sessions and some interracial recordings predate them, the M.G.s were the poster children for racial harmony in Memphis in the turbulent 1960s. When Dunn joined the band in 1965, it was comprised of two black and two white musicians.

M.G.s guitarist Steve Cropper—a tall, well-dressed, bearded man with a ponytail who looks more like a celebrity chef than a guitar hero—took a trip down memory lane with me at his home outside Nashville. On the coffee table in his home outside of Nashville was a toy snowman figure who danced and sang "I'm a Snowman" to the music of "Soul Man," one of many hit records on which Cropper and Dunn performed as session musicians. Cropper recalled, "Duck's brother, Charlie, turned us onto the Plantation Inn when he said, 'There's this great band over in West Memphis.' Of course, we were underage. But Charlie helped sneak us in."

"There was a band over there, a group called the Veltones. They had a lead singer named Sissy Charles. He was awesome and they had this super band, a real R&B blues show band. They did the dance steps. They did flips. They had all the doo-wop harmonies. It was a major show and they played Wednesday through Saturday over there, always the late show on Saturday. You know, it went to two in the morning.

"Sometimes they'd let us in and sometimes they wouldn't. Usually, they'd run us out if a fight broke out because they didn't want to get in trouble if the kids got hurt. There was always some kind of fight going on."[3]

Dunn and Cropper were not the only white suburban teens to feel the effects of WDIA, Daddy-O-Dewey Phillips, and the great black bands at the Plantation Inn. At White Station High School in East Memphis, Sam Phillips's sons, Knox and Jerry, were hanging out with a talented young musician named Jim Dickinson.

Jim Dickinson enjoying a cigar at Zebra Ranch Studio, Coldwater, Mississippi, 2009

Dickinson became an unofficial historian of Memphis music. Except for college in Texas and a short time living in Miami in the 1960s, he spent his whole life and career studying and promoting the city's music.

He once told me that everybody his age learned about music at the Plantation Inn in West Memphis. But young people drinking and partying excessively can sometimes suffer tragic consequences.

★

Carol Feathers was a pretty, redheaded freshman at South Side High School who loved to dance and wanted to become an airline stewardess when she grew up. On Friday night, February 19, 1960, five days before her fifteenth birthday, her twenty-year-old date James Robbins picked her up around 9:00 p.m. James and Carol had known each other for a few months and been on three or four dates.

Richard "Pee Wee" Taylor, nineteen, picked up Pat, his date, and the four friends went to the Cotton Club in West Memphis. Around 2:00 a.m., James Robbins, Pee Wee Taylor, and his date were ready to go home. But Carol Feathers wanted to stay with her best friend, Ann Doyle.

Also there that night was Jerry Blankenship, whom Carol Feathers had known for a few years. They had remained friends after he dropped out of high school and married Patricia Howell, who was pregnant with their first child. Jerry and Patricia were both seventeen. He had steady work as a service station attendant at the Billups Service Station at South Bellevue Boulevard and Orgill Avenue. Their parents lived a few doors apart and the young couple lived with hers at 1115 Beechwood Avenue.

Early that night, Jerry and Patricia Blankenship had fought about money. She wanted him to pay for her two prescriptions for high blood pressure. "If you can't pay five dollars for this medicine, you can just go home," Patricia said.[4]

Jerry Blankenship packed a bag and walked the few doors to his parents' home. But around 10:00 p.m., he got into his 1951 Ford and drove over the bridge to the Cotton Club. Sometime after 2:00 a.m., with Carol Feathers's other friends long departed, Jerry and Carol left the Cotton Club and drove to an abandoned dog track near the bridge.

He was drunk and angry about the earlier fight with his wife. Carol "kind of took a shine to me," said Jerry Blankenship the next day. "I went out to Dacus Lake Road and we parked by the dump.

"Then when I grabbed her, she started fighting. She slapped me and scratched me with her fingernails. The door came open and we fell out on the ground. I picked up a club. I just went out of my head. I hit her a couple of times. I kicked her. Then I dragged her over to a block of concrete. She started fighting again so I hit her again."[5]

Carol Feathers died that night and Jerry Blankenship admitted to the murder the next day. The fact that both were teenagers who should have never been allowed at a nightclub created enough outrage that Danny's and the Cotton Club were permanently closed four days later. The Plantation Inn stayed open until 1964 but no longer allowed teenagers admittance. As a concession to their young patrons, the live music played inside was broadcast through a loudspeaker to the parking lot.

After underage patrons were barred from the Plantation Inn, Jim Dickinson said, "They had a metal, like a drive-in restaurant speaker in the parking lot. You could go and sit in the parking lot and listen to the music."[6]

Don Nix recalled his time at the Plantation Inn: "I would just go and sit and listen to the music. I didn't dance or drink or anything else. I would just sit there and listen to that music."[7]

★

By the time they graduated from Messick High School in 1959, the Royal Spades—which is what Cropper's band called itself—had added his old friend Don Nix on baritone saxophone and West Memphis trumpeter Wayne Jackson.

With Charles "Packy" Axton's access to the fledgling studio owned by his mother and uncle, his friends in the Royal Spades recorded a regional hit in 1961 on their new record label Satellite Records, which later became Stax Records. Titled "Last Night," the record was credited to the young white players and excluded other more seasoned musicians who may have also been on the recording.

Baritone saxophonist Floyd Newman was on that recording session. He was in a band that played at the Plantation Inn and other clubs in

COURTESY OF RICK IVY

The Mar-Keys publicity photo

the region, and he had toured with B.B. King in the early 1950s, after a stint in the U.S. Army. Born in 1931, he was ten years older than most of the members of The Mar-Keys. In our interview, Newman said, "What happened, we were just kind of messin' around at Satellite studio with the band I had at the Plantation Inn, and Gilbert [Caples] and I came up with this blues thing. So Jim [Stewart, the studio owner] said, 'Let's try it.' And we did and it looked like it wasn't going to be put out. But Jim's sister, Mrs. Axton, wanted to put it out. So she pushed it and he released it as by The Mar-Keys. People started calling in for The Mar-Keys. So a band was formed, an all-white band, and sent out on the road as The Mar-Keys. That's what happened."[8]

Steve Cropper disputed that story. "The riff of 'Last Night' started with Jerry Lee 'Smoochy' Smith, keyboard player who played a lot with Chips Moman. Chips had already heard that riff, but Smoochy brought it into the studio one day."[9]

The writer's credit for the song includes Charles "Packy" Axton, producer Chips Moman, Smoochy Smith, and the two Plantation Inn veterans Floyd Newman and Gilbert Caples. The Royal Spades did

COURTESY OF RICK IVY

The Mar-Keys in the studio

change their name to The Mar-Keys. And as The Mar-Keys, they were hired to tour in support of "Last Night," advancing these young musicians from amateur to professional status.

Whatever the truth may be about the origin of "Last Night," the record provided Stax Records with its first success in a nearly two-decade run of great Memphis music.

CHAPTER SIX

THE MEMPHIS BEAT

"If there hadn't been an Elvis, there wouldn't have been The Beatles."

—John Lennon, songwriter, musician

★

By the time the 1960s arrived, many young Memphis musicians who began playing music because of the revolution Elvis started at Sun Records had graduated from high school and were infiltrating local recording studios. A revolving cast of young performers toured as The Mar-Keys, gaining experience and spreading the sound inspired by the Plantation Inn. Music was everywhere locally, and black music was more avidly sought after and publicly embraced by white audiences than ever before.

Elvis Presley had been in and out of the army and was settling into a career making movies. Jerry Lee Lewis's rising star was dimmed by a scandal involving his marriage to his thirteen-year-old cousin. A young senator from Massachusetts named John Fitzgerald Kennedy was energizing a youth movement as a presidential candidate.

By the end of the 1960s, Americans had seen war and three assassinations, civil rights and integration, protests and the summer of love. During that decade, the British Invasion brought America's music back home as filtered through the lenses of young blue-collar English artists.

And the music that sprang from Memphis was part of the soundtrack to it all.

★

The rebellion Elvis began against popular mores inspired a generation of teenagers to create their own approaches to fashion, music, and racial awareness. The next sea change in fashion and music occurred in the mid-1960s and came from Great Britain, led by musicians such as The Beatles and The Rolling Stones who were born into working-class families. Of course, many talented British musicians dominated commercial music in the 1960s, but The Beatles and the Stones have exerted arguably the longest-lasting influence.

The Beatles' first appearance on Ed Sullivan's popular television program on February 9, 1964—much like Elvis Presley's appearance nearly eight years earlier—propelled the British rockers into the forefront of America's awareness. Like with Presley, the hairstyles and clothing of John Lennon, Paul McCartney, George Harrison, and Ringo Starr were considered controversial. And much like in his introduction of Elvis, Sullivan gave The Beatles an important endorsement. On the third of their three consecutive Sunday appearances, on February 23, 1964, he called the band "four of the nicest youngsters we've ever had on the show."[1]

The Beatles and The Rolling Stones were both heavily influenced by American music, including Elvis and the Sun Records roster of artists (Jerry Lee Lewis, Carl Perkins), the Chess Records' bluesmen (Chuck Berry, Muddy Waters), the Motown Records roster, and R&B pioneers such as Little Richard. But it was Elvis who had changed everything for these British musicians.

He had been popular in Memphis and the surrounding area since the summer of 1954. In November 1955, RCA Records purchased Presley's contract from Sun Records with the intention to sell Elvis's music to broader markets, including overseas.

"Heartbreak Hotel" was released in the United States on January 27, 1956. Shortly afterward, Radio Luxembourg included the song on its playlist, introducing Presley's music to a European audience. As John

Lennon once told philosopher Marshall McLuhan, "I heard Elvis Presley. There were a lot of other things going on, but that was the conversion. I kind of dropped everything."[2] He later declared, "If there hadn't been an Elvis, there wouldn't have been The Beatles."[3]

And Stones' guitarist Keith Richards wrote in his autobiography, *Life*, "But the one that really turned me on, like an explosion one night, listening to Radio Luxembourg . . . was 'Heartbreak Hotel.' That was the stunner. I'd never heard of Elvis before. It was almost as if I'd been waiting for it to happen. When I woke up the next day I was a different guy."[4]

Elvis Presley cemented the makeup of future rock and roll bands when he added drums to a lineup that included electric lead guitar, rhythm guitar, and bass. Both The Beatles and The Rolling Stones adopted that core instrumental lineup.

Despite coming from similar socioeconomic backgrounds and sharing an enthusiasm for American roots-based music, The Beatles and The Rolling Stones were very different musically. In the 1950s when they were learning to play, the distance of 175 miles between the future Beatles in Liverpool and the youthful Rolling Stones in London was musically significant.

Skiffle music was a term first coined in the United States in the 1930s to refer to a mixture of blues, black popular music, and boogie-woogie. Harmonically simple, played acoustically, and sometimes including homemade instruments, skiffle had elements of blues, jazz, vaudeville, and folk music in a manner similar to jug bands. The style fell out of favor in the United States but had a resurgence in England in the 1950s. The fact that it was relatively easy to learn and emphasized homemade instruments made it accessible for aspiring low-income musicians. Its leading proponent in Great Britain was Lonnie Donegan, who had a hit with his version of "Rock Island Line," which had been made popular by American folk singer Lead Belly in the late 1930s. The future Beatles got involved with skiffle bands in Liverpool.

The future Stones were listening to and playing American blues with older British musicians in London. Young Mick Jagger, Keith Richards, and Brian Jones frequented a small jazz and blues club there, operated by Alexis Korner. The Rolling Stones aspired to be a blues band, adopting a repertoire and a style exemplified by the electric-guitar-driven sounds of Jimmy Reed and Muddy Waters (whose song "Rollin' Stone" provided the band's name). Elvis Presley's guitarist, Scotty Moore, was another major influence on Keith Richards.

The Beatles' first albums included covers of Sun and Motown hits but also featured early compositions by the songwriting team of John Lennon and Paul McCartney. The Rolling Stones' first albums had covers of songs by American bluesmen Willie Dixon, Chuck Berry, and Jimmy Reed and included some of the first compositions of Mick Jagger and Keith Richards.

These British musicians learned to play in the mid-1950s and were in their late teens and early twenties when they began recording. The first recordings of both bands, before they became global icons, illustrate their influences more clearly than their later, more mature performances. As these artists became more proficient at their craft and had more resources, their music increased in sophistication. Their primary song-writers, Lennon/McCartney and Jagger/Richards, started using different time signatures, instrumentation, and harmonies.

By the mid-1960s, The Beatles, The Rolling Stones, and their contemporaries in Memphis had all heard each other's records and musical cross-pollination had begun. The first Stones album released in the U.S., *England's Newest Hit Makers*, included a version of Memphis singer Rufus Thomas's "Walking the Dog," which had been released on Stax. The Stones later tried to record in Memphis but settled for nearby Muscle Shoals, Alabama, where they enlisted Memphian Jim Dickinson to play piano on the song "Wild Horses." Also hoping to record at Stax Studios, The Beatles had to cancel their sessions due to security concerns. (Don Nix later became close friends with George Harrison and appeared with him at The Concert for Bangladesh in 1971, two shows designed to bring international awareness to the poverty-stricken country.)

At Stax Records, Booker T. & the M.G.s recorded versions of The Beatles' hits "Day Tripper" and "Michelle." They later released an album titled *McLemore Avenue* comprising instrumental renditions of all the songs on The Beatles' *Abbey Road*.

Otis Redding, the most popular artist on the Stax label, recorded a version of "Day Tripper" with Booker T. & the M.G.s, his studio band.

Redding later scored a hit with his intense rendition of the Stones' "(I Can't Get No) Satisfaction."

As Keith Richards wrote in *Life*, "Rhythm and blues was a very important distinction in the '60s. Either you were blues and jazz or you were rock and roll. Rhythm and blues was a term we pounced on because it meant really powerful blues jump bands from Chicago . . . it just depends on how much you lay the backbeat down."[5]

Most blues and rock and roll music is based on 4/4 time, where each bar of music has four equal quarter notes as its basis and is counted one, two, three, four. The Rolling Stones were heavily influenced by Chicago blues, which was usually in 4/4 time with emphasis on the second and fourth beats—commonly called the backbeat. While the backbeat is present in the music of both The Beatles and the Stones (and in almost all of rock music), each beat can be delivered in several ways within the same bar of music. Each single quarter note can be played and divided into an infinite number of possibilities. That's part of the beauty and art of music: the ability to navigate those possibilities differentiates individual musicians and performances.

For example, if each count was one second and divided into a hundred centiseconds, then playing ahead of the beat ("rushing" in musical terms) might be hitting the rhythm at the twenty-fifth centisecond. On top of the beat would be right at the fiftieth centisecond. Behind the beat would be after the fiftieth centisecond. Countless variations on these accents account for part of the distinctive sound of each musician or group. Musicians settle into where within the count they most frequently and comfortably play, also known as the pocket. It can be anywhere within the beat. The pocket was different for The Beatles, The Rolling Stones, and Memphis musicians, distinguishing the feel of their music.

Most members of a band rely on the drummer to set the tempo; that is the heartbeat of the sound of any group. Ringo Starr of The Beatles and Charlie Watts of The Rolling Stones each played a pivotal part in the development of their band's music. Like all good drummers, they set the pocket for the group and made sure that it was unwavering. That freed the instrumentalists and vocalist to interpret the song without consciously worrying about tempo. Like his fellow Beatles, Ringo Starr began playing in skiffle bands, which tended to find the pocket on top of the beat (near the fiftieth centisecond). Charlie Watts, who once aspired to be a jazz drummer, recognized that in the electric blues music favored by the Stones, the beat tended to be slightly later.

Their contemporaneous Memphis musicians were influenced by the first rockers from Sun Records and the black bands they heard at local dances and the Plantation Inn. This confluence of music left an indelible mark on their development, affecting how they played throughout their careers. For generations, black musicians in Memphis found the pocket later in the beat. It is a trait common in Memphis music and can be traced back for decades. An early example is a recording by Williamson's Beale Street Frolic Orchestra from February 27, 1927, called "Bear Wallow Blues." At the time of the recording, the group was the pit band at the historic Palace Theatre on Beale Street. An instrumental, "Bear Wallow Blues" lopes along lazily, seeming about to fall apart rhythmically. It is in time but so far behind the count that the anticipation of the beat keeps the listener engaged and entertained.

One of the most popular songs The Beatles recorded early in their career was 1964's "Twist and Shout," written by Phil Medley and Bert Russell. They performed it with a sense of urgency indicative of truly great rock and roll. John Lennon's vocal was raw and sexy while Ringo Starr's drumming provided a solid beat. It almost sounds rushed, but like the classic skiffle music the young musicians had grown up playing, the pocket is actually just on top of the beat.

In the 1962 Isley Brothers' version of "Twist and Shout," the beat is laid further back and relaxed. Typical of gospel-flavored R&B, this interpretation has the band in the pocket slightly behind the beat. The Beatles' version sounds more like pop music (despite Lennon's raw and sexy vocal) primarily because of where each version laid the pocket.

Jonathan Gould, author of The Beatles biography *Can't Buy Me Love*, wrote that their tendency to play on top of the beat was driven by a love of Motown Records: "With Pete Best on drums, they were restricted to a stomping 4/4 rock and roll beat, and even their attempts at rockabilly lacked any sense of snap, much less swing. When Ringo joined, he brought a rudimentary sense of how to swing the beat, and a fairly nuanced feel for the edgy style of playing that the Motown drummers turned into a high art. So I see the Beatles' tendency to play on top of the beat as mainly derived from their emulation of the Motown rhythm sections and their roots in the headlong groove of Chuck Berry and Little Richard."[6]

The Rolling Stones' version of "Walking the Dog" also has the pocket slightly behind the beat. Rufus Thomas, on his original Stax recording of the song, exemplifies the Memphis sound. Backed by Booker T. & the M.G.s, including Steve Cropper and Duck Dunn, Thomas lets the song fall further back behind the beat than the Rolling Stones allow.

The best way to understand the differences in the pocket between The Rolling Stones, The Beatles, and Booker T. & the M.G.s is to listen to how each band performed the same song. Lennon and McCartney gave an early composition to the Stones to record called "I Wanna Be Your Man," which they later recorded with The Beatles. The Beatles' version is slightly faster and more on top of the beat.

But even after the musicians matured and became more proficient, the pocket didn't change. *Abbey Road*, which The Beatles recorded in 1969, was re-created in total by Booker T. & the M.G.s. in 1970. The difference can be easily heard in the versions of "Come Together": again, the Memphis musicians are laid back in the beat while The Beatles are on top of the count.

Best exemplified by Wilson Pickett's classic "In the Midnight Hour" and led by drummer Al Jackson Jr., the young M.G.s create a tension that resolves each measure by bringing the music together just when it seems as if it may dissolve into chaos. The listener's anticipation of the resolving beat has made the Memphis sound unique for generations.

Al Green explained the tension in our 1978 interview: "It seems like it is off-tempo a little bit, the music and the beat. It seems like it's cluttered a little bit until—right. And you make that roll and *ticka-ticka-ticka-boom*! Bam! Smack you right in the face."[7]

★

Charlie Watts, drummer for The Rolling Stones, was schooled in jazz; Ringo Starr, drummer for The Beatles, began playing skiffle. Terry

Johnson, the drummer for the Royal Spades and later The Mar-Keys, grew up playing country music.

Two years younger than the rest of the group—he met Cropper, Dunn, and Nix as a student at Messick High School—Johnson had experience playing in his father's country band. But he came of age as a musician like many of his cadre of friends: at the Plantation Inn listening to the great black bands around Memphis.

Unlike many of the other revolving members of The Mar-Keys, Johnson did not pursue his career in music. Instead of easing into the local recording scene as fellow young white musicians Steve Cropper, Duck Dunn, Packy Axton, Wayne Jackson, and Charlie Freeman did, he went back to school in the 1960s and earned a PhD in psychology.

The drummer most prevalent on the recording scene in the early 1960s was Al Jackson Jr., who was six years older than most of Packy Axton's circle of friends. Jackson was an established professional musician; he had begun sitting in with his father's big band when he was five years old. By the time he was fourteen, he had a permanent job with his father, Al Jackson Sr., and in other working groups, including Willie Mitchell's band.

The young musicians had heard Jackson at the Plantation Inn and other venues where black bands played for white audiences. They had heard Jackson lay back in the pocket live, but at Stax Records, Jackson made that part of their own musical DNA.

In the early 1960s, The Mar-Keys replaced original members with other musicians as they tired of life on the road. Steve Cropper had left Memphis in the summer of 1961 but returned to work in the newly christened Stax Studios. Recording sessions in Memphis had been integrated for years, and Cropper soon found himself playing with black musicians. Bassist Lewie Steinberg was from a large family of African American musicians dating back to the early 1900s. Howard Grimes was a slightly older black drummer who played with Willie Mitchell and other established musicians. Booker T. Jones was a sixteen-year-old high school baritone saxophonist proficient on a variety of instruments.

After several sessions with that group of musicians, they convinced Booker T. to switch to Hammond B-3 organ and Al Jackson Jr. to join the rhythm section. Grimes had been Jackson's disciple and played in a similar style. Eventually, Cropper's high school classmate Duck Dunn replaced Lewie Steinberg and the lineup of Booker T. & the M.G.s was set.

Cropper remembered those days in my interview with him: "We were fortunate enough to get Al Jackson on some sessions. We had Howard Grimes, almost on a regular basis, a great drummer. But every time Jackson came, it was just something a little extra. It was something a little more magic. Jim Stewart and I would look at each other and say, 'Man, that Al Jackson. He's just unbelievable. We've got to get him.'

"Well, his loyalty to Willie Mitchell made it difficult. We tried and tried. Al says, 'No, I don't want a steady job. I'm playing at night with Willie and I'm doing this recording over there at Hi.' We finally convinced him to come over on a regular basis."[8]

Jackson was a member of Willie Mitchell's touring band and had been a regular on recording sessions for the producer at Hi Records. When Jackson came to Stax, an arrangement was made to allow him to continue to record for Hi. It was not unusual for the best session musicians to work at multiple studios and for different labels.

Booker T. & the M.G.s at the Overton Park Shell, June 1969

Willie Mitchell told me in 1977, "Most of the time, I would have Al Jackson and Howard Grimes around. And if one of them didn't feel something, they would just turn it over to the other guy. Sometimes one would play on this tune and the other one play on another tune."[9]

By the mid-1960s, this lineup of Booker T. & the M.G.s was set with white musicians Steve Cropper and Duck Dunn playing with black musicians Booker T. Jones and Al Jackson Jr. They became the regular house band on Stax Records sessions. Former Mar-Keys members Wayne Jackson and Packy Axton were regulars on sessions all over Memphis. Don Nix was established as a producer at Stax where he helmed the historic sessions for bluesman Albert King's *Born Under a Bad Sign* album.

The commingling of white suburban kids and black inner-city musicians was complete. Soul music from Memphis spread across the planet seeping into the collective consciousness of established contemporary music.

Asa Carter's worst fears had been realized. Music had brought "people of both races together."[10]

CHAPTER SEVEN

GHOSTS WALKED AMONG THEM

"The blues shows were great in that it was a very public forum where black people and white people could kind of share musical ideas and say we are all culturally linked. We're all going somewhere."

—Sid Selvidge, singer, musician

★

Ralph Peer was a talent scout for the RCA Victor Phonograph Company in the 1920s. In 1927, armed with a portable recorder, he visited Bristol in eastern Tennessee. He discovered and recorded several artists, including Jimmie Rodgers, aka the Singing Brakeman, and the Carter family. Those sessions are considered the beginning of modern country music.

The same year, Peer went to several other Southern cities, including Memphis, to record local talent. He learned of Will Shade, Ishman Bracey, and Walter "Furry" Lewis, among several others. Although these musicians lived in the city, their style of music was dubbed "country blues." They were usually solo or duo acts with acoustic guitars, the occasional mandolin, and vocals. Jug bands were larger and featured a variety of unusual instruments in addition to guitars: washboards, kazoos, tub bass, and, of course, jugs, which made a low humming noise.

After some success in the late 1920s, the "race music" market, black blues music sold mainly to African Americans, diminished when the Great Depression hit in 1929. Despite having a wooden leg, Walter "Furry" Lewis took a job sweeping the streets of Memphis. He kept that job for thirty-six years. Largely forgotten and relegated to poverty, the country bluesmen struggled, unaware of their place in America's musical history. In 1959, a book by Samuel Charters titled *The Country Blues* was published and it began a resurgence of interest in these older artists.

★

In the early 1960s, Packy Axton and his bandmates infiltrated his family's recording studio. Once The Mar-Keys' song "Last Night" became a hit, their path was set: they would record R&B music at Stax, which they had learned from the older Plantation Inn musicians.

A number of other white Memphis high school kids inspired by the first generation of rockers at Sam Phillips's studio were not part of the scene at Stax. They also went to West Memphis to hear the great black bands but took a different route in bringing African American elements to their music.

The so-called Beat Generation spread with the 1957 publication of Jack Kerouac's novel *On the Road* and musical groups like The Weavers. Folk music gained favor with college kids in the late 1950s, culminating in Bob Dylan's eponymous debut album in 1962, which legitimized protest songs for a wider market. In the early 1960s, coffee shops drew crowds of folk music devotees in Memphis and other cities.

As far as young musicians, such as Jim Dickinson and Sid Selvidge, knew, country blues artists were ghosts. Then Samuel Charters's book revealed that the ghosts still walked among them.

When historian Pete Daniel went to visit Jim Dickinson for an interview in 1992, Jim shared these memories: "*The Country Blues*, the Sam Charters book, was the first time I realized some of these men are still alive, and not only are they still alive, they're down the street. A friend of mine and I followed the trail that Charters left to Gus Cannon, who was the first one I actually met. He was somebody's yard man at the time.

CARLEEN DORIAN PALMER

Gus Cannon at the Beale Street Music Festival, Memphis, May 1977

Gus told this family that he used to make records and was on RCA. And they'd say, 'Yeah, Gus, sure. Cut the grass.'

"When we met him, he was bending down over the lawn mower. He had just been cutting the grass. He lived on the property at the back over a garage, and he took us up into his room. On the wall, he had a certificate for a million sales from BMI for *Walk Right In*."[1]

Don Nix, one of The Mar-Keys and a frequent presence at Stax, said, "I never associated Furry's blues with Ben Branch or Willie Mitchell. I thought it was too folk music or folk blues, not realizing that R&B came from guys like Furry and Bukka White and all of those old blues singers. . . . The thing that brought all that together in Memphis was a kind of beatnik Bohemian coffee shop called the Bitter Lemon. They would hire these old blues singers."[2]

A transplanted Mississippian named Charles Elmer, who called himself Charlie Brown, started the Bitter Lemon. He realized that the bluesmen Charters wrote about in *The Country Blues* were still alive and in Memphis. He and his cohorts began locating these blues pioneers and paying them to perform. Several successfully started a second career as a result of their reentry into live music. Blues legends like Mississippi John Hurt, Sleepy John Estes, Bukka White, and Furry Lewis played the Bitter Lemon, a venue as important to the development of Memphis musicians in the 1960s as the Plantation Inn had been in the 1950s.

Once the connection between country blues and the R&B played at the Plantation Inn became clear to young Memphis musicians, they incorporated some of the older repertoire into their performances. This was happening at roughly the same time in Great Britain and other places where aspiring artists were discovering R&B and the country blues through records. English bands like Eric Clapton–led Cream, Led Zeppelin, and, of course, The Rolling Stones all repurposed country blues songs into mega-selling records.

Walter "Furry" Lewis at Memphis Music Exhibit, Brooks Memorial Art Gallery, Memphis, September 2, 1976

The difference between learning from records in a foreign land and directly from the creators of this music is huge. In the same manner as R&B, which area teens learned in West Memphis as local music, the country blues was legitimate folk music, passed on in an oral tradition from one artist to another.

Furry Lewis was especially important to this new generation of musicians. He took an interest and befriended many in his youthful audience. Singer and guitarist Sid Selvidge, a fixture in Memphis music, recorded several acclaimed albums and was a regular at the Bitter Lemon. He shared these memories with me during an interview in 2000: "My major recollection of the Bitter Lemon was Furry Lewis. It was an epiphany. I can remember being at the Bitter Lemon and seeing Furry playing one night. I had never seen him before and it just blew me away. He played slide and I had never seen anybody do that in person.

"Furry was a great, great singer. But what he could do with his voice was so melodic and where he went with it. And that he could do it and play guitar at the same time. I was just fascinated.

"At that point, I wanted to be Furry Lewis. And that was probably the biggest change musically in my life."[3]

★

After absorbing the influences of the black bands in West Memphis and melding that with the country bluesmen, young white rockers who had begun as Elvis Presley acolytes were developing their musical identities. It made sense to spread the word and showcase these newly rediscovered blues heroes.

In 1966, a group of friends who frequented the Bitter Lemon presented the first Memphis Country Blues Festival at the Overton Park Shell, a bandstand built in the 1930s to present classical music and light opera. The festival continued through the 1960s, bringing awareness of Memphis's blues heritage to the community.

The early blues festivals featured legendary performers Bukka White, Sleepy John Estes, Gus Cannon, Furry Lewis, and Reverend Robert Wilkins alongside young white musicians like Sid Selvidge, Lee Baker, Jim Dickinson, and music writer Robert Palmer's band The Insect Trust.

COURTESY OF RICK IVY

FOURTH ANNUAL MEMPHIS COUNTRY BLUES FESTIVAL

(all shows except Sunday night will be held at the Shell in Overton Park--Sunday night show will be held in Mid-South Coliseum)

Friday, June 6th--11 a.m. Showcase: brief appearances by Canned Heat, Winter, and many of the other artists are appearing later in the Festival: plus top country blues talent

8 p.m. Focus on Country Blues with Bukka White, Furry Lewis, Nathan Beauregard, Fred McDowell and Johnny Woods, Sleepy John Estes, plus Johnny Winter and many others

Saturday, June 7th--11 a.m. Blues performers young and old including John Fahey, Jo Ann Kelly, Robinsonville Five, Johnny Woods, many others

8 p.m. Electric Blues with Canned Heat, Moloch, Insect Trust, Piano Red, and many others

Sunday June 8th 1--3 p.m. Gospel Program with Elder MacIntorsh and Henry Speller, Rev. Robert Wilkins, the Maxwell Singers, Soldiers of the Cross and many others.

(Coliseum) 5 p.m. First Annual W. C. Handy Memorial Concert. The headliners: Booker T. and the MG's, Albert King, The World's Greatest Jazzband, Carla Thomas, The Bar-Kays, Rufus Thomas, Cassietta George, Sun Smith and his Beale Street Band, Bukka White and other top performers.

THE FIRST ANNUAL W.C. HANDY MEMORIAL CONCERT SPONSORED BY MEMPHIS SESQUICENTENNIAL, INC.

Memphis Country Blues Festival lineup, June 6–8, 1969

Jimmy Crosthwait served as the master of ceremonies and played washboard with some of the acts.

When the first Memphis Country Blues Festival was produced in 1966, I was fourteen years old. My friend Rick Ivy and I got a ride to Overton Park where we hung around backstage and met Furry Lewis for the first time. It was an eye-opener for two kids from the all-white suburbs. We went every year they presented a festival.

Sid Selvidge explained, "The blues shows were great in that it was a very public forum where black people and white people could kind of share musical ideas and say we are all culturally linked. We're all going somewhere."[4]

As rock music festivals became a national phenomenon following the highly visible one in Woodstock, New York, in 1969, the blues festivals in Memphis ended. They were followed by a series of festivals and shows at the Overton Park Shell lasting until the 1990s. The venue has been renamed the Levitt Shell and hosts 50 free concerts annually.

"Upon arrival, we checked into the Linden Lodge on Beale Street and found that we had been placed last on the list for the show." Blues/rock band ZZ Top front man Billy Gibbons said about playing a later festival at the Overton Park Shell in the early 1970s. "Following the show, we were greeted by the local leaders in the rock scene — Jim Dickinson, Lee Baker, Robert Johnson, the Ardent crew, all the important players on the scene! It was following subsequent visits through town that took us to Ardent Studios. After that, we knew where we wanted to be: Memphis."[5]

★

Jim Dickinson had played on several sessions for Jerry Wexler at Atlantic Records and was an in-demand keyboardist. He produced or played with Ry Cooder, The Rolling Stones, Aretha Franklin, Arlo Guthrie, and many others.

Warner Bros. Brothers Records offered him a development deal: he recorded acts at their expense, which upon approval led to a contract. He decided to form a band comprised of musicians he had worked with both at the Bitter Lemon and at the Memphis Country Blues Festivals. Unlike the other Plantation Inn acolytes who began recording a decade earlier at Stax, such as Steve Cropper and Duck Dunn, these artists had refined their music to include the sounds of country blues.

Sid Selvidge recalled, "Mud Boy and the Neutrons was basically Jim's idea. We had all met at the Bitter Lemon. Jim Dickinson, Jimmy Crosthwait, Lee Baker, and myself. Jim was making headway in the music business at the time as a producer. He had some connections with Warner Bros.' president Lenny Waronker and he had a development deal.

"He had been working with Ry Cooder, and Ry was talking about some band and said, 'I don't know who they are. It could be Mud Boy and the Neutrons for all I know.' And Dickinson said, 'Can I use that?'"[6]

The recording sessions did not result in a contract from Warner Bros., but the band became a local favorite. As the band's popularity grew, artist John McIntire sculpted a piece representing Mud Boy in clay from the Mississippi River. It is featured on the cover of an LP titled *Known Felons in Drag* released on France's New Rose Records. Mud Boy and the Neutrons continued playing in Memphis until guitarist Lee Baker was murdered in 1996.

Selvidge recalled the spiritual aspirations of Mud Boy and the Neutrons. "We were four people who, if we played together right, Mud Boy would rise up out of the Mississippi and everybody would be happy. When we played for the audience, the music had to be so good and so Memphis that Mud Boy would actually rise up out of the river."[7]

CHAPTER EIGHT

CITY MICE AND COUNTRY MICE

"If you were black for one Saturday night on Beale Street,
never would you want to be white again."
 —Rufus Thomas, the world's oldest teenager,
  in *All Day and All Night*

★

Rufus Thomas, the late singer, comedian, master of ceremonies, and patriarch of a musical family in Memphis, spent years hanging out and working on iconic Beale Street beginning in the 1930s. After urban renewal gentrified the street in the 1980s, he was awarded a parking spot near the corner of Beale and Hernando Streets in recognition of his long association with the historic entertainment district.

Often called "Black America's Main Street," Beale was the center of commerce and entertainment for African Americans in Memphis and the surrounding area from the late nineteenth century until the 1970s. During the daytime hours, the street was busy with shoppers, pawnbrokers, fruit stands, photographers, dance instructors, dentists, and other medical providers. It was the place that black people from Memphis and the surrounding areas could go for their everyday needs.

In the evenings, it was a thriving entertainment nexus for farmers and rubes, gamblers and con men, and African Americans looking for an evening out. Although the real estate was mostly owned by Italians, the street catered to the black community, and it was wide open for illegal activities by a population that had seen subjugation and oppression for generations.

It had begun as a destination for recreation when barge workers and roustabouts docked where the street meets the Mississippi River. From there, they made the short walk up to the whorehouses, gambling saloons, and joints around Beale.

Beale Street legends are plentiful. Some may have even be true. Allegedly, W.C. Handy wrote the lyrics to "The Memphis Blues" at the cigar stand at Pee Wee's Saloon, which was open twenty-four hours a day. Blues great Furry Lewis once joked, "They tied the key around a rabbit's neck. Couldn't catch the rabbit so they never could close."[1] Elvis Presley

179 Beale Street, abandoned dentist office next to a boarded up pool hall, 1976

CARLEEN DORIAN PALMER

was rumored to have played at Club Handy in the 1950s. And each morning, the undertaker removed dead bodies from the alleys behind Beale.

★

Wild Bill Latura was a white family man—and a cold-blooded murderer. He had three adorable children (daughters Rose Virginia, Allie Elizabeth, and Dorothy Mae), a wife named Allie, and a thriving business selling hamburgers from stands he owned around Memphis in the early twentieth century. He ground the meat at his home on the east side of Dunlap Street near Poplar Avenue; his father had a grocery store on the corner. A large hamburger at one of Latura's stands cost five cents. He eventually opened a saloon attached to the store on Dunlap.

An acquaintance of Latura named Dan Wright went to the saloon on August 8, 1902, a typical summer day. Wright, who had recently been let go from the fire department, had a violent disposition. At Latura's saloon, Wright was offered a free beer. Since it was a hot day, he wanted another, and the bartender graciously treated Wright to three beers on the house.

When he was refused a fourth, words were exchanged and a fight broke out between the ex-firefighter and saloon employees. Latura pulled out his baseball bat and used it to fracture Dan Wright's skull. Wright was the first person Latura killed. He was not prosecuted since he had corroborating witnesses who called it self-defense.

However, this family man had trouble with the law over the next few years, including a series of knife fights, the last in March 1908, during which he received a long gash that scarred down his right jawline. Latura didn't only use knives, though—by that time, he had already shot three people. And on December 10, 1908, Latura committed an act of murder heinous enough to inscribe him infamously into Beale Street lore.

Hammitt Ashford's saloon, which catered to black clientele, was on the northwest corner of Beale and Fourth Streets. Although white establishments at that time were off-limits to blacks, the reverse was not the case. Like most saloons on Beale Street in the turn of the last century, Hammitt Ashford sold drinks and had gambling in a back room, as well as pool tables that were always busy. Considered one of the finer establishments, the saloon's regular clientele included men and women of various social strata who simply enjoyed an evening out. Latura had several black friends and frequented Hammitt Ashford's to gamble. He liked to gamble but was not considered a good loser, which was unfortunate since he often lost.

Just before midnight on that Thursday evening, he had a particularly bad night gambling. Wild Bill Latura supposedly told an acquaintance, "Damn those old niggers has won away all of my money. I'm going home and get my gun and I'm coming back here and make a funeral parlor out of this place."[2]

As he entered the saloon, he told the bartender he was going back to the washroom. He walked into the poolroom, unbuttoned his coat, drew his .38 caliber pistol, and began shooting at black men playing billiards at the first table by the back wall. Bob "Speck" Carter was his first victim, followed by Charles "Long Boy" Miller, then Clarence "Candy" Allen and Leslie Williams. Speck Carter, Long Boy Miller, and Candy Allen died almost instantly. Williams survived being shot in the hip. Latura wounded two more people before he was done: Richard Scot and Birdie Hines, who was shot trying to shield her companion. On Latura's way out of the bar, he pointed his weapon at another black patron and told him not to move or he would shoot him as well.

Latura then strolled up Beale past a Chinese restaurant toward Third Street. He turned right at Hernando Street, disposed of his gun, and went to Rosebud's saloon at the corner of Hernando and Gayoso Avenue to enjoy a drink. Latura's close friend Punch Wilson entered Hammitt Ashford's saloon and, seeing the carnage, immediately left to join his friend at Rosebud's. The pair were picked up at Rosebud's and taken to jail. Latura said, "I just shot 'em and that's all there is to it."[3]

The next day, Bill Latura faced a grand jury, pleaded not guilty, and was held without bond. He was charged with three murders plus three attempted murders, and Punch Wilson was charged as an accessory after the fact.

His case took a long time to come to trial—Latura spent two years in jail before an all-white jury found him not guilty due to insanity. Dr. W.B. Sanford diagnosed him with "progressive paranoia." He was just twenty-eight years old and was referred to as "Wild Bill" in the local newspaper.

In 1912, after his release for the murders, Latura warned the editor of the *Commercial Appeal*, C.P.J. Mooney, to stop calling him Wild Bill or he would shoot up the newsroom and kill the entire editorial staff. The writers were ordered not to use the name Wild Bill in future reports. Boyce House, a young reporter unaware of the threat, joined the staff of the *Commercial Appeal* in 1915. One August day, he wrote that "Wild Bill Latura" could be considered one of the city's tourist attractions. Reading this, Latura was furious and promised revenge on the reporter and newspaper.

The area of Memphis that included Bill Latura's saloon was patrolled by Officers Charlie Davis and John "Sandy" Lyons. Although liquor had been banned in Tennessee for six years, the laws had rarely been enforced. After Latura threatened local law enforcement in mid-August, Officers Davis and Lyons were told by their superiors that they would be fined ten days pay if Latura continued selling alcohol. The raid of Latura's saloon by Davis and Lyons yielded more than a thousand bottles of beer and prompted an additional threat from Latura against Police Chief Oliver Perry and Captain John Couch.

On a muggy Saturday night, the day after the article about the raid appeared in the *Commercial Appeal*, Officers Davis and Lyons approached Latura's stand from the Dunlap side. When Latura saw them, he accosted them and said they were scaring his employees and threatened to kill them.

"Bill, you're under arrest," said Officer Lyons. Wild Bill reached toward his pocket and Lyons shot him four times. A pistol fell out of Latura's pocket as he staggered across Dunlap, fell, and lay bleeding in the street just outside his place. The *News Scimitar*, local rival of the *Commercial Appeal*, reported, "Bleeding and gasping for breath, he lay in the street without attention from a group of spectators . . . they were afraid to touch him fearing he might be shamming. His twelve-year-old daughter Rose saw him dying in the street and rushed over to him."[4]

Wild Bill Latura died at City Hospital that evening. John "Sandy" Lyons was arrested but cleared of all charges.

★

In his book *Where I Was Born and Raised*, David Cohn wrote, "The Mississippi Delta begins in the lobby of the Peabody Hotel in Memphis and ends on Catfish Row in Vicksburg."⁵ He was referring to the Delta of the landed gentry who frequented the Peabody, located two blocks north of Beale Street. There they could enjoy luxury accommodations, dining, and entertainment. If the landed gentry's Delta began in the hotel a few blocks north, the intersection of the Delta's rural and Memphis's urban music was on Beale.

Evening activities were not just confined to Beale Street but included the surrounding areas. Streets on either side were lined with restaurants, houses of prostitution, and nightlife. Johnny Mills had a famous barbecue place on Fourth Street near Beale, and Culpepper's Barbecue was on Hernando. Both attracted large crowds, including celebrities in town staying at the Peabody Hotel.

As the largest city in the region, country people from three states (Tennessee, Arkansas, and Mississippi) came to Memphis to shop, sell their produce, and find entertainment. Often, these rural visitors had a rude awakening to city life.

John "Peter" Chatman was professionally known as Memphis Slim. He began his career as a pianist in Memphis and later found an international following as a blues musician. We spoke in 1978 when he visited Memphis from his longtime home in Paris. A tall, well-dressed man with a white streak down the center of his hair, Slim described some of the interactions of rural patrons on Beale Street in the 1930s.

"At Second and Beale, they had a place they called the wagon yard. They actually came in with their wagons and their mules. And some of them had trucks. They'd park it right back there, that's why they called it the wagon yard. . . . Soon as they gin their cotton, they would want to go to Beale Street. And they go up and down Beale Street."

He described crooked games of chance in which country folks lost most of the money they had made selling their wares. Much like in the fable of the country mouse, things usually did not end well for them.

"We robbed them and take their money. Their watch and things like that," remembered Memphis Slim. "And the police would say, 'What the hell. Beale Street, what do you expect? We told you not to go down there. Hell, I'm scared to go down there myself.'"[6]

★

Maurice "Fess" Hulbert was born in 1896 in Crawfordsville, Mississippi; he moved to Memphis in 1921 to live with his grandmother, after he'd spent a short time in St. Louis. Over the next few decades, he witnessed the rise and fall of Beale Street as a patron and an entrepreneur.

In the 1920s, he opened the first black dance studio in Memphis called the Palm Garden, which was upstairs on the southeast corner of Fourth and Beale Streets. They taught ballroom dancing as well as current dances such as the Cootie Crawl and the Black Box. The studio was popular, and word spread about their talented young dancers.

"We built a balcony in our ballroom for all the white people to come up there," Hulbert said during my interview with him in 1979, "because white folks and black folks didn't mix together too much."[7]

He was operating a printing press when we spoke in 1979. We sat in his crowded office just off Beale surrounded by a mixture of flyers, posters, and other print jobs, alongside photos from his remarkable career.

After his success with the Palm Garden and a few other studios around town, Hulbert became a Beale Street restaurateur, promoter, and band leader. By the 1930s, Fess Hulbert was booking bands into his ballroom on Beale, which changed names frequently. "Every time we'd change the name, we'd renew it, redecorate it, and give it a new name. And we'd draw a better crowd. Every time."[8]

The Palm Garden was variously known as the Oriental and the Paradise. Regular performers included Ethel Waters and former Memphian-made-good Jimmie Lunceford. Hulbert booked Louis Armstrong just up the street at the Palace Theatre and in the 1940s led his own band called Hulbert's Lo-Down Hounds.

He started in the restaurant business in the early 1930s by opening the Ritz, which had orchestral music at lunch and dinner. According to Hulbert, the Ritz had "table cards, napkins, and was real ritzy,"[9] but there was a counter on the other side where patrons could get a hot dog for a dime.

But Beale Street was wide open to gambling, prostitution, and con men, and regulars didn't just go for the hot dogs. Most saloons had an established tradition of gambling in the back. Some had piano players in the front room, and all could signal the gamblers when police showed up.

"I had a great big place with tables all around," said Hulbert. "All had Pokeno boards and I had sawdust on the ground. In the middle of my place, I had canvas, stretched canvas, and jukeboxes. They would dance to the music of the jukebox and play Pokeno. But now, you have to go all the way to the back to the Pokeno room. The outside was open. And, of course, if the police came in, I touched my buzzer, and we signal everybody out back that the police was coming. And when the police got back there, we always kept a mug of beer or a soft drink or something on the table. And when the police come, they don't see nothing." The glasses created the illusion that patrons were just enjoying a casual drink instead of gambling.

Hulbert continued, "They'd take the Pokeno boards and drop them off of the tables and hide them in the sawdust. So when the police get back there, they couldn't see. Everything would be clear."[10]

★

Prior to 1940, Beale Street catered to patrons by offering three distinct musical styles rooted in blues: the more sophisticated multi-instrumental music played in concert venues, the country blues for those who enjoyed guitarists or jug bands in the parks or on the street corner, and the barrelhouse boogie pianists who played mostly as background in the gambling joints that lined the street.

Nationally prominent African American musical acts often performed at the Church Park Auditorium. Located on Beale just east of Fourth Street, it held more than 2,000 people and often presented touring bands of schooled musicians reading music from charts. Many of these more popular out-of-town bands stayed at Mickey Clark's Hotel, near the corner of Beale and Second Streets.

Beale Street theaters, including the Palace, were located between Hernando and Fourth Streets and presented music, dance, and comedy.

Vaudeville-type shows often included tap dancers, comedic routines, and a revue of female dancers, such as Harlem in Havana or the Brown Skin Beauties. Fess Hulbert's ballrooms showcased established black musicians.

In the 1930s, Charlie Williamson had the pit band at the Palace Theatre serving as the musical accompaniment for local and out-of-town artists. According to band member Thomas Pinkston, the Williamson group "was the greatest Negro show band in the world then."[11]

Delta blues musicians and jug bands found new audiences and the opportunity to earn tip money by performing in the parks and streets around Beale. Rural musicians could make more money with their guitars in Memphis than working at hard labor in the surrounding countryside. The jug bands were primarily a product of city dwellers who used unconventional instruments like kazoos, washtub bass, and jugs as part of their musical lexicon. They played to the rural people visiting Beale Street and walking in the parks.

And inside the joints on Beale, pianists played to crowds typically more interested in the gambling activities in the backrooms or at the bar. With inventive nicknames like Slopjar, Dishrag, and Turnip Greens, these musicians often incorporated jazz and blues into a more sophisticated sound than that offered on the street by their rural counterparts.

The history of Beale Street as an entertainment destination had distinct eras. The first was wide open to gambling, prostitution, and other vices that were overlooked by police. This lasted until 1940 when Edward Hull "Boss" Crump ordered it cleaned up. The second was as a haven for jazz, and finally, Beale Street became a gentrified entertainment district filled with bars and restaurants catering primarily to tourists.

History has not recorded a definitive reason for Crump's actions and many theories abound. I always heard that he made a deal with the U.S. Navy to open a base in nearby Millington on land that had been owned by the government since 1920. Allegedly, the reputation of Beale Street, as permissive of gambling, prostitution, and violence, was a major issue for the safety of naval personnel. The base brought jobs and money to the region, and Crump agreed to clean up the district before the Navy would commit to the project. The cleanup began in the spring of 1940.

And in February 1942, the naval Shore Station Development Board recommended approval of the base in Millington.

After Crump's police commissioner, "Holy Joe" Boyle, closed the houses of prostitution and gambling joints, the street became a home for jazz musicians and a more sophisticated black audience.

This post–"Holy Joe" era for Beale Street is an important chapter in the story of jazz in Memphis. A number of significant jazz artists who graduated from the city schools in the 1940s and 1950s honed their skills on Beale. It was an important breeding ground for Memphis music.

CHAPTER NINE

JAZZ: TEACHERS AND STUDENTS

"Before I left New York, I had tryouts for the band and that's where I got all those Memphis musicians—Coleman, Strozier, and Mabern. (They had gone to school with the great young trumpet player Booker Little . . . I wonder what they were doing down there when all them guys came through that one school.)"

—Miles Davis, jazz icon

★

Jazz music, much like blues, can be traced to the early days of the twentieth century and many consider it an offshoot of the blues. As mentioned earlier, W.C. Handy and Buddy Bolden, touchstones for blues and jazz, were probably similar in terms of repertoire and instrumentation.

In Memphis, Chicago, Philadelphia, New York, Los Angeles, and other cities that had vibrant jazz scenes, the lines were sometimes blurred between blues, gospel, and jazz. Often unable to sustain a living outside of New York City, many musicians who aspired to play jazz had to be proficient in many styles.

Charlie Williamson's band at the Palace Theatre on Beale Street backed up local and visiting singers without categorization. Thomas Pinkston, who played in Williamson's Palace Theatre pit band, recalled,

"We'd play for Ethel Waters, Mamie Smith, Bessie Smith, Ida Cox, Sara Martin, and others."[1]

There are many great early Memphis contributors to the jazz world besides W.C. Handy and Jimmie Lunceford. From 1929 to 1939, Memphian Gene Gifford was the principal arranger for the Casa Loma Orchestra, one of the most popular white big bands of that time.

Along with Pinkston, one of Handy's sidemen was William "Buster" Bailey who, as a fifteen-year-old, played clarinet in the Memphis band in the 1910s. Shortly afterward, he met Louis Armstrong when he joined New Orleans jazzman King Oliver's Creole Jazz Band. He later refined his arranging skills as a member of the Fletcher Henderson Orchestra in the 1920s. Lil Hardin was raised in Memphis, moved to Chicago, married Louis Armstrong, and joined his band as a pianist and arranger. Another Memphian, Johnny Dunn, one of the most influential trumpeters of the early 1920s, was rumored to have been improvising before or at the same time as Armstrong.

Mary Lou Williams, considered one of the twentieth century's greatest jazz pianists and arrangers, was a child prodigy. In 1922, at the age of twelve, she performed with Duke Ellington's small band. She married saxophonist John Williams in 1926 and joined his five-piece combo, the Syncopators. The couple moved the group from Chicago to Memphis before John joined Andy Kirk and His Twelve Clouds of Joy in Oklahoma City in 1929. Mary Lou kept the Syncopators active in Memphis for a few years until she joined her husband in Andy Kirk's band.

★

There was a tradition of big bands that included two generations of one family. Bassist Al Jackson included his namesake son on drums when Al Jr. was fourteen; Phineas Newborn did the same for his sons, pianist Phineas Jr. and guitarist Calvin.

Legend has it that a small black boy wandered into the O.K. Houck & Co. music store one day. Barely tall enough to reach the keyboard, he began playing the sheet music. He became a regular there, voraciously devouring all the printed music at Houck's. People kept telling Phineas Newborn, a drummer and bandleader, about the boy. But he was not looking for a new pianist for his band. Then one day, he happened into the store to see his son standing at the piano. Phineas Jr. was the piano prodigy that everyone was talking about. At the age of fifteen, Phineas Newborn Jr. joined his father's band, followed by his brother guitarist Calvin and Calvin's wife, Wanda, who played trombone and sang. The Newborn family band played the Plantation Inn during the 1940s and early 1950s.

The Steinberg family bands included several siblings: Luther, Morris, Wilber, and Lewie. Their indoctrination to music came from their father, who was a pianist at Pee Wee's Saloon on Beale Street.

Starting with the big bands in the 1920s, jazz was often dance music. Young patrons of the music wanted to dance. That message carried weight at the local level in many cities across the world. Memphis bands played popular tunes and arrangements for dancing for both black and white audiences. The complex and sophisticated arrangements of the bands of Duke Ellington, Fletcher Henderson, Benny Goodman, and others required skilled musicians to read music from charts. They elevated big band music while still retaining the dance aspects. Their scores are still studied and replicated by contemporary groups in concert halls and on college campuses.

In the 1940s, the music went from the dance halls to small night clubs when bebop, a new style of jazz, was introduced in New York. Honed by jazz musicians in after-hours clubs, bebop was a sophisticated musical form with looser rhythms, improvised extended solos, and complex harmonies. It was music meant for listening rather than dancing, often played late at night following more traditional big band performances. The shellac used in manufacturing 78 rpm records became more available after World War II, and bebop was heard outside the clubs in New York through records.

Bebop emerged at a time when a few important developments were occurring that affected Memphis music. The first was the 1940 cleanup of prostitution, gambling, and hustlers on Beale Street. After a few years, social activity on the street became safer and more accessible to black Memphis audiences looking for an evening free of those unsavory activities. Several new music venues opened, including Club Handy and the

Flamingo Club. Hotel Men's Improvement Club, located just off Beale, was operated by waiters from the Peabody Hotel.

Andrew Chaplin was the drummer in Jimmie Lunceford's Chickasaw Syncopators. He remembered the Hotel Men's Improvement Club on Beale during our 1993 interview: "Well, see at the Hotel Men's, the waiters ran it and that was their club. That's where they'd have their meetings and they'd rent it out. I remember Bennie Moten brought his band there. Fletcher Henderson brought a band in there. And then we'd play in there and all of the local bands would play in the Hotel Men's Improvement Club."[2]

Wednesday nights at the Palace Theatre were designated Amateur Night on Beale Street, with host Rufus Thomas, who welcomed white patrons. Future stars, including B.B. King, Bobby "Blue" Bland, and Johnny Ace, competed for prizes and the opportunity to launch their careers.

Of course, nightlife flourished in other sections of Memphis as well. Clubs like the Brown Derby in Orange Mound and Currie's Club

CARLEEN DORIAN PALMER

B.B. King at the Beale Street Music Festival, Memphis, May 1977

Tropicana in North Memphis all featured live entertainment. White-only nightclubs like the Silver Slipper, Bucket of Blood, and the Eagle's Nest also showcased music.

But Andrew "Sunbeam" Mitchell's Club Handy on Beale Street was the most significant as an after-hours venue. Bebop flourished there, and it's where musicians went after an evening's work to relax and experiment.

★

In Memphis, music education in schools for African Americans began in the 1920s when gym teacher Jimmie Lunceford started the city's first school band at Manassas High School. It was continued in the 1940s by Professor W.T. McDaniel, who alternated his teaching between Manassas and Booker T. Washington schools. Two new high schools, Melrose and Douglass, opened in 1938, bringing the number of black high schools to four.

Students at these high schools, encouraged by their band instructors, embraced the freedom of this new music. The schools turned out a high number of kids proficient enough on their instruments to create a large pool of musicians capable of playing bebop. Their mix of youthful exuberance and sophisticated instruction, beginning in the neighborhoods and continuing in the schools, yielded some of the most talented and influential jazz musicians assembled outside of the jazz capitals (New York, Los Angeles, Chicago, and Philadelphia).

It was in this era that baritone saxophonist Fred Ford graduated from Douglass High School and trumpeter Willie Mitchell from Melrose. A group of future stars, including George Coleman, Frank Strozier, Charles Lloyd, Harold Mabern, and Hank Crawford, graduated from Manassas. And Floyd Newman, Phineas Newborn Jr., and his brother Calvin graduated from Booker T. Washington High School.

Miles Davis remembered meeting some of these Memphis high graduates in his autobiography: "Before I left New York, I had tryouts for the band and that's where I got all those Memphis musicians—Coleman, Strozier, and Mabern. (They had gone to school with the great young trumpet player Booker Little . . . I wonder what they were doing down there when all them guys came through that one school?)"[3]

★

Phineas Newborn Jr. checked all the boxes for a great Memphis jazz musician. He studied with Professor McDaniel, came from a musical family who started him playing professionally as a teenager, spent after-hours jamming at Club Handy, and had a successful career as a working jazzman in New York. But Phineas Jr. was different than the other future jazz stars who went through the Memphis high schools: he was a genius.

According to his lifelong friend Fred Ford, when Phineas Jr. entered Tennessee State University, he was given sight-reading tests to judge his prowess for the band. Phineas Jr. read everything put in front of him. Then he turned the pages upside down and played the music upside down and backward.

After years of playing and recording in Memphis, Phineas Jr. made a name for himself in jazz circles, moving to New York in 1956 at the behest of Count Basie. He made several acclaimed albums for Atlantic Records and RCA Records, among others.

In his liner notes for Phineas's album *The Great Jazz Piano of Phineas Newborn Jr.*, renowned jazz critic Leonard Feather is quoted: "It would not be extravagant to claim that Phineas has no equal among American jazz pianists, from any standpoint, technical, or esthetic."[4] In his liner notes to Phineas's *Please Send Me Someone to Love*, Feather wrote, "Newborn is the greatest living jazz pianist."[5]

Phineas Newborn Jr. had a successful recording and touring career during the second half of the 1950s before mental illness caused him to be briefly hospitalized in 1958. He relocated to Los Angeles around 1960, recording several more albums before having a second mental breakdown. This time, he was institutionalized for several years. Returning to Memphis, he moved in with his mother and played a few local shows.

In 1974, Newborn went into Ardent Studios and recorded *Solo Piano*, a Grammy-nominated album, for Atlantic Records. It confirmed Phineas Newborn Jr.'s status as one of the most gifted pianists of his generation. He lived the rest of his life in Memphis, playing publicly occasionally, and he continued to suffer from mental illness until his death in 1989.

Phineas Newborn Jr. at the Beale Street Music Festival, Memphis, May 1983

ERICA DUNCAN

★

Young musicians well schooled on their instruments coupled with new venues created a golden age for Memphis bebop. Club Handy, on the second floor above an apothecary, was the eye of the hurricane.

The life of a traveling musician was never easy, especially in the days before the Civil Rights Act of 1964, which ended segregation in public places. Even popular African American artists suffered from a lack of hotels willing to house black musicians and unscrupulous promoters who would short them or withhold pay.

Early African American touring bands stayed at Mickey Clarks's hotel on Beale Street or at a rooming house run by Sade Bugs on Driver Street. Andrew "Sunbeam" Mitchell and his wife, Ernestine, opened Mitchell's Hotel in 1943 to accommodate traveling musicians. Located in the former Citizen's Club, the Mitchells named their establishment Mitchell's Hotel and Lounge. They were initially prohibited from presenting live music because of a city ordinance. Once they were able to have music in the venue, they changed the name to Domino Lounge and then finally to Club Handy.

Mitchell's Hotel was famous for extending credit to musicians who were stranded in Memphis between gigs. I interviewed Sunbeam Mitchell in 1979 in his office at Club Paradise. Filled with mementos from his long career, he regaled me with stories of the hotel and clubs he operated.

"Little Richard, Roy Brown, and just any of the old big names stopped at Mitchell's Hotel. We had a name [reputation] when musicians come in and get stranded. Well, we had a thing I wouldn't say a soup line, but we was to cater to having a chili. And we could sell to people for thirty-five cents a bowl. My wife did that."[6]

Jackie Wilson, Ike and Tina Turner, and B.B. King all appeared at Club Handy. Mitchell often presented up-and-coming R&B acts in the tiny room on the second floor above the drugstore and later at his show-case venue, Club Paradise. When the cavernous Club Paradise opened in 1964 in a room that was built as a bowling alley, Chester Burnett, aka Howlin' Wolf, was the first act to perform and Count Basie played at the official opening.

Club Handy was an after-hours stop for young hip musicians who wanted to test their skills against one another. Jam sessions started late and often continued until early morning. It was not unusual to find a mix of local and out-of-town musicians pushing each other artistically. Cutting contests, aka cutting sessions, had been common in jazz circles since the 1930s. These often began with the band playing a standard song known to everyone. After the theme, soloists would take turns improvising, using the harmonic structure of the song as a basis. They sometimes used parts of the melody as references within the solo, or they might restate the entire theme while changing the rhythm or melody.

Tenor saxophonist Bill Harvey led the band at Club Handy. An older established professional, Harvey mentored the young jazzmen just graduating from high school. His band was legendary and included a rarity—a woman saxophonist, Evelyn "The Whip" Young. The group later served as B.B. King's first touring band in the 1950s. Harvey was so beloved that after he lost his leg to diabetes, a benefit concert was planned to buy him a prosthetic one.

"He went to the hospital and he had his leg taken off. He'd had sugar [diabetes]," Sunbeam Mitchell explained to me. "They tried to raise money to get him a leg after he was out of the hospital. But during the time, they never did get it off the ground to raise benefits for him to get a leg. And he passed before they could get anything done."[7]

According to Club Handy regular Willie Mitchell, "Bill Harvey was something like the father of all of the musicians. Everybody would hang around him because he knew music. He was a good arranger, and if he saw some talent, he would always try to put it together. Plus he was a good player."[8]

To understand how this group of future jazz stars developed so rapidly after high school requires an appreciation for the elements that shaped them. They all came under the guidance of great high school band directors like Professor McDaniel, Matt Garrett, Andy Goodrich, Emerson Able, and Onzie Horne, who taught them to read music. Those teachers also took some students on engagements to demonstrate how to behave like a professional musician.

Because they could read music and had some professional experience, these high schoolers were offered jobs with more polished players.

Howard Yancey, a booking agent on Beale Street, often used them in a larger band with more expensive established musicians to save money. They usually played parties or early evening shows.

Finally, Club Handy's Bill Harvey taught the kids all the standard tunes and introduced them to the nuance of harmony and improvisation.

"We'd play tunes like 'Cherokee,' 'What Is This Thing Called Love?' 'All the Things You Are.' Just all of the standard tunes," saxophonist Fred Ford remembered. "The jazz musicians took George Gershwin's tunes and a lot of other composers, and they made jazz classics out of those tunes."[9]

W.T. McDaniel and others were important as band instructors, but the students needed practical guidance from Bill Harvey at Club Handy. Harvey died of complications from diabetes with scant recognition of his legacy and contributions to recorded music.

"Bill Harvey had schooled all of us on all of these so-called standards," recalled Emerson Able. "We would play until everybody had his chance to either cut somebody's head or let somebody embarrass them. You just play until your stuff starts sounding bad to you, or somebody would just come up and just push you out of the way and start playing. . . . The problem was trying to keep a drummer alive so he could continuously play while these other guys solo."[10]

★

Whenever I spoke to Phineas Newborn Jr., I felt like there was another conversation going on in his head that excluded me. He was always amiable and engaging. I surmised that the other conversation was musical and never-ending.

In the mid-1980s, I was the corporate director of entertainment for the Peabody Hotel. Like many luxury hotels, we had a lobby bar with a grand piano. I would sometimes receive a telephone call late at night from hotel security.

"Sorry to bother you so late, but Phineas Newborn Jr. is playing piano in the lobby and he won't leave. What should we do?"

My response was always the same: "Just leave him alone and enjoy what he's playing."

CHAPTER TEN

BOOKER AND DOUGHBELLY

"When you hear music, after it's over, it's gone, in the air. You can never capture it again."
—Eric Dolphy, jazz musician

★

Jazz legend Eric Dolphy uttered these words following a performance in Hilversum, Holland, in 1964. The sentiment was sadly true for the music of two artists who got their start in the black high schools in Memphis. Dolphy's bandmate Booker Little Jr. and saxophonist Leonard "Doughbelly" Campbell were brilliant musicians who each died before they were twenty-four years old.

About ten years separated the two: Little was born on April 2, 1938, Campbell most likely in 1928. Both saw action in the after-hours cutting sessions at Club Handy, although not contemporaneously.

Despite dying at only age twenty-three, on October 5, 1961, from a blood disorder called uremic poisoning, Booker Little Jr. is still revered in jazz circles. He began his studies at Manassas High School under W.T. McDaniel but transferred to the Chicago Conservancy in 1954 during his sophomore year. Little was born into a musical family that included a trombonist father and church organist mother. He had three sisters, one of whom became an opera singer in London, Germany, and Italy.

Little moved to New York City, the jazz epicenter of the world, in the late 1950s and immediately entered the elite realm of the avant-garde. Considered one of the bright new talents on trumpet, he made several recordings as a band leader and sometimes as a musician within other ensembles. He started with the Max Roach Quintet and later recorded or appeared live with Slide Hampton, Sonny Stitt, Abbey Lincoln, Mal Waldron, and others.

The rhythmic and harmonic freedom of bebop expanded in the late 1950s thanks to the emergence of avant-garde jazz under the influence of innovators including John Coltrane, Ornette Coleman, Cecil Taylor, and Eric Dolphy. Little's training at the Chicago Conservancy gave him a background in classical music that gained him entrée to work with Coltrane and Dolphy. Booker moved freely within the bebop and avant-garde jazz circles.

In an interview with *Metronome* magazine in 1961, Little shared, "There are a lot of people who think the new direction should be to abolish form, and others who feel that it should be to unite the classical forms with jazz. There's so many areas of trumpet playing that can be employed, and they don't have a lot to do with the 'legitimate' end of trumpet playing as such. There are a lot of notes between notes—they call them 'quarter-tones.' They're not really quarter-tones but notes that are above and below."[1] Little was referring to the diatonic scale, which is the basis of Western standard harmony.

Some of Booker's challenging compositions are still in the jazz repertoire. According to influential jazz critic Nat Hentoff, "Had he lived long enough to develop a body of work, he would have unquestionably been regarded as among the most durably original of jazz composers."[2]

Booker Little died too young. Although he has an extensive recorded output, he was poised to become a major innovator in jazz. His recordings, both as a leader and especially with Eric Dolphy and Charles Mingus, are among the staples of avant-garde jazz.

★

The entrance to Club Handy, above the Pantaze Apothecary on the corner of Lauderdale and Beale Street, was through a side door. A mirror hung on the back wall at the top of the stairs where Bill Harvey could usually be seen reflected, as he played on the bandstand with an array of saxophonists and trumpeters all trying to best one another with long solos.

Opposite the top landing was a small bandstand in the far corner of the dimly lit room. The writer Stanley Booth told me that the dim lighting made cigarette smoke appear green. This was Club Handy in the 1940s and 1950s, and it was home to the city's hip music loving after-hours crowd. The room was small and usually crowded. The tiny stage at Club Handy was always full, especially during after-hours cutting sessions. Fabric hanging over the stage diffused the music, improving the sound for both audience and musicians.

On the stage, the band could be playing a standard tune, each soloist trying to best the last and discourage the next from coming to the bandstand. A rotating set of pianists sometimes included Charles Thomas, Phineas Newborn Jr., and Manny Dell.

The small dark room was often full of musicians arriving from their gigs, dropping by to cut loose and enjoy the music. When a short round man with a tenor sax took the stage, all the saxophonists except Bill Harvey left the bandstand.

Leonard "Doughbelly" Campbell owned the stage at Club Handy. His solos were powerful, his technique flawless. This was his house and everybody knew it. Out-of-town musicians who came by to test themselves against this incendiary young player soon discovered the truth behind the legend.

Willie Mitchell recalled, "He was waiting for all of the [Count] Basie players and the best of the saxophone players because he was going to skin their head when they get there."[3]

★

Tuff Green, like many of the African American school bandleaders, often used students in his group. Among them, Leonard "Doughbelly" Campbell was special. Everybody knew it. He often got the call from Green for performances, both while Campbell was in high school and after his graduation.

Green led his own band for years. Musicians had come and gone, including Phineas Newborn, the drummer father of talented pianist Phineas Newborn Jr. and his brother Calvin. Newborn Sr. formed his own family group after a stint in Tuff Green's band. In early 1950s, Nat King Cole, the most popular black performer in America, asked Tuff Green's band to back him up at the Million Dollar Theatre in Los Angeles. It was a big break for Green's band, and Doughbelly was on board for the trip.

Perhaps the most famous cutting sessions in jazz history were between tenor saxophonists Dexter Gordon and Wardell Gray, both based in Los Angeles in the 1940s. Their saxophone battles were legendary. Gray's fluid melodic style contrasted with Gordon's more jagged intense phrasing. Their recording of "The Chase" was one of the best live recorded examples of a classic cutting session. According to Gordon, "There'd be a lot of cats on the stand, but by the end of the session, it would wind up with Wardell and myself."[4] These sessions typically were held after-hours in the jazz clubs on Central Avenue where Doughbelly often sat in after his shows with Nat King Cole.

Driving back from their Los Angeles engagement in February 1950, Tuff Green's drummer Marcellous Dern fell asleep at the wheel. Both Dern and Leonard "Doughbelly" Campbell were killed. Doughbelly was only twenty-one years old.

Unlike Booker Little who left an exhaustive recorded legacy, Doughbelly's stunning ability is a legend based on the recollections of those who heard him play. Like Little, he was poised to become a major voice in jazz.

Years later, sax man Fred Ford recalled meeting Wardell Gray in Los Angeles: "Every morning at Doughbelly's hotel room, Wardell Gray would be sitting there saying, 'Please play for me, let me hear you play just a cappella.'"[5]

Quoting Gray, Ford continued, "I've never heard anybody play a tenor saxophone like that, including Coleman Hawkins and Don Byas. He was going to go down in history as one of the greatest that ever lived. All that man had to do was just live."[6]

★

Nobel Prize–winning author Aleksandr Solzhenitsyn wrote in a poem, "Some are bound to die young. By dying young a man stays young forever in people's memory. If he burns brightly before he dies, his light shines for all time."[7]

No one knows what the future held for Booker Little and Leonard "Doughbelly" Campbell. But their lights shone brightly during the short time they had.

CHAPTER ELEVEN

SAINTS AND SINNERS

*"If you have it in your heart, then the blues and the spiritu-
als serve the same purpose."*
—Bobby "Blue" Bland, blues singer

★

Before the war between the states was fought, in part, over the
abolishment of slavery, white and black people sought redemption
together at large gatherings called camp meetings. In July 1800 in
Logan County, Kentucky, the first American camp meeting took
place near the Gaspar River Church. Prior to that meeting, traveling
preachers had gone on horseback to small communities to spread the
word of Christianity.

Often associated with the Methodist Church, the camp meeting
movement may have started with Presbyterian minister Reverend
James McGready. At its zenith in the 1830s and 1840s, camp meetings
drew crowds of up to 20,000, including blacks and whites across several
denominations. Attendees at camp meetings would involuntarily fall
into a dance-like trance, a phenomenon known as jerking. In 1801 at
the Cane Ridge Revival, 3,000 people fell to the ground in a swoon of
religious ecstasy and were carried to a facility close by to recover.[1]

The meetings continued until the dawn of the Civil War, when a divided country discontinued race-mixing activities. Camp meetings were the first large-scale interracial attempt to save the soul of the nation.

★

There has always been a tenuous relationship between the blues, the so-called devil's music, and gospel music. While the subject matter was vastly different, the music and instrumentation were sometimes similar. When former blues singer Thomas "Georgia Tom" Dorsey began writing gospel music in the 1930s, he used sacred themes and blues-based music.

For many years, artists crossed this line. Bluesman Robert Wilkins became Reverend Robert Wilkins. Gary Davis became Reverend Gary Davis. And after a successful career as a soul singer, Memphian Al Green founded the Full Gospel Tabernacle Church and became Reverend Al Green. There are numerous instances throughout the twentieth century of African American musicians abandoning secular music for the church.

Several prominent gospel artists had careers in secular music, usually soul music of the 1960s and 1970s. Sam Cooke and the gospel group The

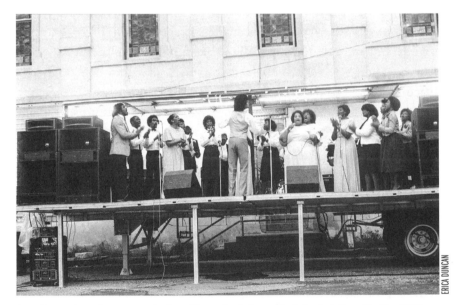

Gospel group in performance at the Gospel Stage, Beale Street Music Festival, Memphis, May 1983

Staple Singers, whose patriarch Roebuck "Pops" Staples began his career as a bluesman, are examples of the crossover of the genres.

Countless musicians, both black and white who played in various styles, cited church music among their early influences. Booker Little's father played trombone in the church where his mother was the organist. Soul saxophonist Andrew Love, a member of the famed Memphis Horns, had a preacher father and a mother who played piano in her husband's church.

Gospel music's influence on Elvis Presley has been well documented. He recorded religious albums, and The Jordanaires, a popular quartet, were his background singers. Although there were distinct lines between church and secular music, so-called saints and sinners, most artists were able to reconcile the differences.

★

Jerry Lee Lewis, who was one of the originators of rock and roll, was also discovered by record producer Sam Phillips, just like Elvis. Raised in a religious family, Lewis learned to play piano in church and attended Southwestern Assemblies of God University in Waxahachie, Texas. His cousin Jimmy Swaggart was a well-known preacher who had a successful career as a televangelist.

Lewis was tormented by the conflict between secular and church music. While preparing for a recording session at Sun Studio, he had the following conversation on October 8, 1957, with Phillips. Here are some excerpts from their debate before recording "Great Balls of Fire," one of rock and roll's seminal records.

> Jerry Lee Lewis: H-E-L-L. Good God almighty, great balls of fire. It says, "Make merry with the joy of God only." But when it comes to worldly music, rock and roll, anything like that, you're in the world and you haven't come from out of the world. And you're still a sinner . . . unless you be saved and born again and be made as a little child. And walk before God and be holy. And brother, I mean you gotta be so pure,

and no sin shall enter there. No sin! . . . It don't say just a little bit. It says, "No sin shall enter there." Brother, not one little bit. You gotta walk and talk with God to go to heaven. You've got to be so good to enter heaven. Hallelujah.

Sam Phillips: All right, you're right. Look, Jerry, religious conviction doesn't mean anything resembling extremism. . . . You mean to tell me that you're gonna take the Bible, that you're gonna take God's word—and you're gonna revolutionize the whole universe? Now listen, Jesus Christ was sent here by God Almighty. Did he save all the people in the world?

JLL: No, but he tried to.

SP: He sure did. Jesus Christ came into this world. He tolerated youth. He didn't speak from one pulpit. He went around and did better for everyone.

JLL: That's right! He went everywhere. He preached on land. . . . He preached on water. And then he done everything. He healed. . . .

SP: Now here's the difference. . . . Jesus Christ, in my opinion, is just as real today as he was when he came into this world. . . . I'm telling you out of my heart and I've studied the Bible. . . .

JLL: I have, too. Through and through. And I know what I'm talking about.

SP: You think that you can't do good as far as rock and roll is formed.

JLL: You can do good. Don't get me wrong, Mr. Phillips. . . . You can have a kind heart. . . . You can help people.

SP: You can save souls.

JLL: No, no, no. How can the devil save souls? . . . What are you talking about? Man, there's the devil in me. If I didn't have, I'd be a Christian. . . . Mr. Phillips, I don't care . . . it ain't what you believe, it's what's written in the Bible![2]

Lewis, believing he was on the wrong side of God and headed to hell, then recorded "Great Balls of Fire." It was one of the most popular early rock and roll songs, heard by millions of young people.

Jerry Lee had been expelled from Southwestern Assemblies of God University after performing a boogie-woogie version of "My God Is Real" at a talent show. He later ran into Pearry Green, the president of the student body, who asked if he was still playing devil's music. Lewis replied that he was, and that the same music that got him kicked out of school is the kind of music they perform in their churches today. The difference, according to Lewis, is he knew that he was playing for the devil and they didn't.

★

One of the best known and most prolific early gospel songwriters was Memphian Lucie Campbell, born in 1885 to former slaves in Duck Hill, Mississippi. She was an educator and composer of more than a hundred songs, including "The Lord Is My Shepherd," "He'll Understand and Say Well Done," and "The King's Highway."

According to ethnomusicologist Bill Ellis, "Alongside such musical peers as Thomas A. Dorsey, Roberta Martin, and fellow Memphian Reverend W. Herbert Brewster, she helped forge the black gospel sound of the first half of the twentieth century and belongs to a small coterie of composers who have set lasting standards for religious music in the black Baptist church."[3]

★

In 1907, Charles Harrison Mason founded the Church of God in Christ (COGIC) in Memphis. It grew into a major denomination with more than twelve thousand churches and six million followers. It had a significant influence on church music and earned its place as a bedrock for American music.

Religious music for rural and urban church members unaccustomed to musical trends or popular songs tended to be easy to follow in the early twentieth century. Before the widespread introduction of recording

RICK IVY

Gospel star Rance Allen in performance, Memphis, December 1978

technology, sheet music was the principal means of distributing songs. But reproducing music from written pages required a skilled reader, instruments, and often a leader.

Singing could occur at any time in a COGIC service and sometimes lasted for several hours. The music was central to the service and was not only considered a gift of the Holy Spirit but also inspired by God through the Holy Spirit. Everyone, regardless of musical ability, was invited to participate. Instrumentation unique to COGIC in the early twentieth century sometimes included piano, trombone, trumpet, saxophone, drums, tambourines, triangles, mandolins, and ukulele.[4]

Born in Texas around 1889, a young blind woman named Juanita Drane, also known as Arizona Dranes, joined COGIC sometime in the early 1920s. She began playing piano in the church, introducing elements of popular music using a strong left-handed pattern associated with ragtime and boogie. In those styles, the pianist plays a repeated bass line in the lower registers with the left hand and the chords and melody with the right. Beginning in 1926, she made several popular recordings in Chicago considered by many to be the first gospel records. Her influence turned traditionally staid religious singing into a looser, more spontaneous style with a barrelhouse piano accompaniment. Dranes opened the door for Sister Rosetta Tharpe, another COGIC member.

Although Tharpe was about twenty-five years younger, their careers in gospel music began at almost the same time. Born in 1915 in Cotton Plant, Arkansas, about eighty miles from Memphis, six-year-old Rosetta (née Nubin) accompanied her mother's singing and preaching performances on guitar. At age nineteen, Rosetta married a COGIC preacher named Thomas Thorpe, adopted a variation of his last name, and became Sister Rosetta Tharpe. Her mark on gospel music was significant. She revolutionized the guitar sounds heard in religious music with her use of distortion. She took gospel music onto the concert stage and introduced it to a larger audience by playing often with secular bands. But her greatest fame came as an influence on rock musicians both in the United States and England.

Tharpe, who began recording in 1938, crossed the line between secular and sacred music. Her virtuoso guitar-playing and rollicking stage presence was a precursor to rock and roll. Sister Rosetta was a beacon to early rockers like Little Richard, Elvis Presley, and Jerry Lee Lewis.

In 1963, she toured Europe, making an appearance in Manchester, England, with bluesman Muddy Waters. British blues guitarists Jeff Beck, Keith Richards, and Eric Clapton credited that show as a major influence on their styles.

★

It was a Sunday morning in 1979 at the Full Gospel Tabernacle Church around the corner from Elvis Presley's Graceland Mansion. But it wasn't a typical worship service: a French crew was there to film the charismatic young preacher, and the place was lit like a Hollywood movie set.

The band began to play, the choir started their call-and-response singing, and from a door behind the pulpit emerged the lean, muscular preacher dressed in a three-piece white suit. He had the demeanor of a rock star because he had been one. Reverend Al Green, recently converted from his life of fame and fortune, was there to lead the service at this Memphis church.

Parishioners began to sway to the music. The band's tempo was building, and the choir seemed energized as they called on the Holy Spirit. Men and women swooned and fell to the floor, much like the jerking at nineteenth-century camp meetings.

Despite the heat from the lights, a young woman in a three-quarter-length fur coat came to the pulpit to sing "Amazing Grace" a cappella.

RICK IVY

Reverend Al Green in his Full Gospel Tabernacle Church, Memphis, December 1978

New to the assembly, her name was Ruby Wilson and her rendition of the classic spiritual was chilling.

The French film crew looked overwhelmed, ready to run for the door at any moment. The congregants' religious fervor must have been unsettling to the foreigners expecting to film a pop star in an environment more staid than a Southern black church service presided over by Reverend Green.

I was assigned by *DownBeat* magazine to do a feature story on Al Green's conversion to gospel. In 1979, it was a rarity for white people to intrude on black church services, but the reverend invited me to come with my photographer. Heathen that I was, I planned to escape out the back door after a few hours. Two things made this impossible. First, my photographer and I were the only white people (outside of the French film crew) in the church, making any escape noticeable. Second, Reverend Green, whom I had known for a few years, pointed in my direction and said, "I see my friend David Less is here with us today."

Services could last up to six hours with Reverend Green never stopping for a break. White handkerchief in hand, he stomped and pleaded with parishioners to accept Jesus and abandon sin. What seemed to me to be headed for chaos moments before was now totally in Green's control; the congregation hung on his every word.

The French filmmakers tried to get Reverend Green to stay in frame by frantically waving their arms in the direction they wanted him to go. Invariably, he moved in the opposite direction. I don't think he was purposefully being difficult. But when he was in his element, it was incumbent on them to catch him, not the other way around.

I knew Green from his time as a pop superstar in the early 1970s and had seen him perform his secular hits at a show on August 31, 1973, at the Memphis Mid-South Coliseum, an eleven thousand-seat venue. His control of that audience was much the same as in his small church. Wherever he pointed in the crowd, people literally swooned.

At that concert, the audience predictably stood to dance on their seats or in the open area in front of the stage. Security ran to the front of the stage and announced that the show would end unless everyone got back in their seats. Once his fans were seated, Green performed one of his biggest hits, "I Can't Get Next to You." Two security guards stood in front of the stage to keep that area clear. It seemed as if out of chaos, order had been restored.

Visibly annoyed by the intrusion, Green took his microphone to the front edge of the stage, still singing his hit. "I just can't get next to you," he crooned. Then he inserted the line, "Because if I was you, I wouldn't let nothing stop you from getting next to me."

At that point, the two panicked security guards quickly moved out of the way as the crowd rushed the stage. Green's control of the audience was Svengali-like. They were there for him; anything he wanted was possible. He evoked that same feeling in his church services.

Al Green has been successful as a soul singer and religious leader by bringing the same charisma and audience interplay in both roles. It was the same way that Sam Phillips charmed Jerry Lee Lewis into recording one of rock's pivotal songs. The best religious leaders are able to tap into that skill to reach their audience.

The difference between sacred and secular music is the yin and yang of the Memphis sound. Like Bobby "Blue" Bland once said, "If you have it in your heart, then the blues and the spirituals serve the same purpose."[5]

CHAPTER TWELVE

HEADS OR TAILS OR . . .

"They talk about Jews and the niggers. They can say what they want about us, but we are the backbone of this country."
—Thomas Pinkston, musician, author

★

Jews and blacks and whites and Southerners and Yankees: varying degrees of love and hate existed among these groups based on geography and social order and historical animosities.

The stain of slavery and hundreds of years of oppression separates Southern whites and blacks. While some people think of slavery as ancient history, I personally knew a man whose parents were enslaved. I also knew others whose grandparents were slaves or fought in the Civil War. The reason for the war has been debated (slavery or states' rights), but whatever the impetus, a divided country was reunited under duress. The South lost, and as with all losing crusades, the victors dictated the terms of surrender. Naturally, soldiers trying to kill one another would not establish cordial relations because of an armistice. Many Southerners suffered under the Yankees' reconstructionist policies.

If there is a caste system in Memphis for blacks and whites, Southerners and Yankees, then Jews land somewhere toward the bottom. My ancestors had no role in the Civil War. They arrived in America from Russia and Poland around the turn of the twentieth century. Not immune to the hatred lingering after the Civil War, family lore tells of the Ku Klux Klan burning my grandparents' Arkansas home and business in the 1920s.

On August 11 and 12, 2017, a group called Unite the Right staged a rally in Charlottesville, Virginia. Ostensibly, a gathering to protest the removal of Confederate war monuments, the march filled up with neo-Nazis, white supremacists, and Ku Klux Klansmen. It was the first time in twenty-first-century America that hate groups based on race, religion, and geography had such a public stage. Chanting racist and anti-Semitic slogans ("Jews will not replace us"), the rally turned violent when counterprotesters and the hate groups clashed. A young woman from the opposition protesters was killed when a car driven by a Unite the Right member purposely plowed into a crowd.

The situation was exacerbated when President Donald Trump refused to condemn the "alt-right," infamously declaring, "You also had people that were very fine people on both sides."[1] Sherrilyn Ifill, president of the NAACP's Legal Defense and Educational Fund, tweeted that Trump had advanced a moral equivalency between racists and their opponents. Former Virginia congressman Eric Cantor, a Southern conservative and a Jewish Republican, called Trump's comments unacceptable.

★

Atlantic Records co-owner and legendary record producer Jerry Wexler once told me, "It's the old vulgar [saying], 'A Jew ain't nothing but a nigger inside out.'"[2] Although Judaism is a religion and includes all races, Jews are often vilified by hate mongers and considered in a separate caste regardless of race.

Early black bluesmen often cited a lack of other work opportunities as the impetus for becoming a musician. They could choose to get up early and work in the fields or play music, sleep late, and entertain at picnics and parties. Either way, no one was getting rich. The same lack of opportunity plagued early immigrants, especially Jews, in the South. So it makes sense that the story of Memphis music includes a cadre of Jewish musicians. Sammy Gould, Berl Olswanger, and Marvin Stamm were some of the more prominent twentieth-century Jewish Memphis musicians.

In considering the racial collision that occurred in the city's music, if white musicians represented heads on a coin, and African Americans tails, Jewish musicians represented the coin standing on its edge.

★

When we spoke in 1979, Nate Evans was seventy-six years old and had been part of the Memphis music scene since the 1910s. He made his way into his living room and sat in a recliner that appeared molded to his body. White flight had long since decimated this once-upscale midtown section of Memphis known as the "Jew Ghetto," but Evans and his wife remained in their comfortable two-story home. The "Jew Ghetto" had been my childhood neighborhood until my parents, concerned about integration, moved in 1962.

Baron Hirsch, the Orthodox synagogue, was the center of Jewish life and the reason for the density of Jewish homes in the area from the 1950s until the 1980s. It opened a new satellite facility in the former East Memphis home of Stax Records artist Isaac Hayes as black people began to move into the area in the 1960s. By 1988, it closed the site near Evans's home and built a new synagogue attached to the former Hayes house.

Relaxing in his recliner, Nate Evans described the life of a professional white musician in Memphis during the early twentieth century. Evans's family moved to Memphis from New York in 1915 when Nate was twelve years old. His mother started him on the violin at a young age, and he began playing professionally as a teenager. Classically trained, he was in demand for string quartets as well as society and dance bands.

At a society function at Tech High School, he met a like-minded young violinist named Sammy Lazarov. They became lifelong friends, sometimes sharing the stage and often substituting for each other. As teenagers, Lazarov took violin lessons from William Saxby, and Nate studied with Joseph Cortese.

"There were three Cortese brothers. And they were all artists," said Evans. "There was Jack, who played flute. Angelo played harp, and Joe played the violin. The society people paid through the nose to get their services. They played for weddings and funerals."[3]

Although the Corteses were favorite performers for early twentieth-century Memphis high society, as Italians and Catholics, they were outside of that social group. Joe was willing to give lessons to Evans, who was Jewish. He also taught Thomas Pinkston, an African American violinist.

Thomas Pinkston described the circumstances of his studying with Joe Cortese during my interview with him the week before his seventy-ninth birthday in 1978: "I played the violin all my life. And I got to where I could play it fairly well. . . . A fellow named Walters, white fellow, worked at O.K. Houck's music store. He heard me playing it and he said, 'How would you like to go on further and study?' I said, 'I'd like it.'

"And he got a man named Mr. Cortese. Well, this man told him to bring me up to his studio at Third and Jefferson."[4]

As a result, Joe Cortese taught Nate Evans, a Jewish musician, and Thomas Pinkston, an African American. The teenagers' paths ran parallel many times over the next sixty years, but they apparently never met.

Beginning in 1915, before W.C. Handy moved to New York in 1918, his Memphis band included fifteen-year-old violinist Thomas Pinkston. He most likely played the Alaskan Roof Garden shows with Handy's band. At the same time, Nate Evans, also an adolescent violinist, was beginning to find work with white bands.

"There was a roof garden called the Alaskan Roof Garden on top of the Falls Building," Evans explained. "And first, W.C. Handy and his band played up there for two or three seasons. He was followed by Malcolm Burke Band, which was a white band. His number-one violinist was Johnny Scruggs. Number two was Sammy Lazarov, when Johnny wasn't available. And when neither one of them were available, they called me. I played up there with Malcolm Burke several times."[5]

In the 1920s, Pinkston joined Williamson's Beale Street Frolic Orchestra in the pit band at the historic Palace Theatre at Fourth and Beale. During that same time, Evans was in the pit band at the Orpheum Theatre down the street at Beale and Main.

Jewish composers and musicians borrowed from African Americans throughout the twentieth century. From George Gershwin to Benny

Goodman, Sophie Tucker to Al Jolson, Jewish artists appropriated black musical traditions. Some of the earliest inroads of black music into the white lexicon was through Jewish performers.

★

There must be something about old men and their recliners. Just as Nate Evans's recliner seemed to envelop him, Thomas Pinkston wore his chair like a comfortable jacket. Both men had been integral to certain aspects of Memphis music. Interviewing them in the same year helped me understand Wexler's conflation that "a Jew ain't nothing but a nigger inside out."

From an early age, I had a passion for African American culture and music that matured in the late 1960s during the vogue of black hipness. In the mid-1970s, I began researching Memphis music under a Younger Scholars grant from the National Endowment for the Humanities. There was scant information available, and most of the work that had been done earlier focused on blues music and rural areas surrounding Memphis.

Naturally, the opportunity to interview a member of W.C. Handy's Memphis band was exciting. Thomas Pinkston was bright, articulate, and had a wealth of information about his fellow members in the band. He told me stories about Beale Street and the music made there. Then the conversation changed from music to race. His views on race and politics were unconventional, to say the least.

"Mr. Handy told me once, 'Let nobody fool you. With all the strikes against you, the United States is the greatest place in the world for anybody.'" Pinkston sat up in his chair as he spoke to me. "We got the Ku Klux killing us. Why don't we go back to Africa? . . . I'm glad they brought my ancestry over here, because I've acquired your ways of living, your knowledge, and everything. Just to think, I'd be sitting up over in Africa barefooted with that diaper on, eating a banana hollering 'boola boola' if they'd left me in Africa."

His voice rose as he made his point. "But since they brought my ancestors to this country, I'm quite proud. Because the American white man and the American Negro are two of the most respected figures on

Earth. Ain't nobody beat the United States doing nothing. They might try. I'm grateful for them bringing me over. I'll tell you like I told a bunch of Jews out there. I don't know whether you're Jewish."

I replied that I was Jewish.

"They talk about Jews and the niggers. They can say what they want about us, but we are the backbone of this country."[6]

CHAPTER THIRTEEN

SAM PHILLIPS AND THE BIRTH OF ROCK AND ROLL

"And even though he was black, it wasn't rhythm and blues and it wasn't rock and roll, 'cause there wasn't such a thing."
—Sam Phillips, record producer

★

As the video crew from the Smithsonian Institution was setting up the room for my interview with Sam Phillips's protégé Jack Clement, we spoke privately at the top of the stairs leading into the studio. I asked Jack a rather tongue-in-cheek question.

"Do you know when Sam went mad?"

To my surprise, Clement gave me a specific date. It was the occasion of Phillips's second nervous breakdown and subsequent shock treatment.

"It seems significant," I told Clement, "because if it preceded his invention of rock and roll, then rock and roll was the product of a madman. If it followed, then rock and roll could drive you mad."[1]

Clement gave a date that was earlier than when Sam Phillips ushered in rock and roll with the first recordings of Elvis Presley. In truth, rock and roll may be the product of someone who crossed the line between psychotic and genius.

★

SMITHSONIAN INSTITUTION ARCHIVES, ACCESSION 11-009, IMAGE #92-5359 #27. PHOTO BY PETE DANIEL

Sam Phillips at home in
Memphis, Tennessee,
May 1992

Sam Phillips led the way for Memphis producers for generations. For
a white businessman in the early 1950s, he had an unusual affinity for
black music. Attuned to the artistry and commercial potential of rural
musicians, Phillips's oeuvre includes first recordings of significant
twentieth-century blues artists.

Blues music, aka race music, began to be recorded in the 1920s primarily for an African American audience. With little feel for the music,
the always-white producers focused mainly on the technical aspects of
capturing the acoustic performances.

By the time Sam Phillips opened his Memphis Recording Service
studio at 706 Union Avenue on January 3, 1950, electric instruments
and larger groups were prevalent. His experience with radio, particularly in setting up the big band broadcasts at the Peabody Hotel, gave
him the technical skills needed to capture the sounds he wanted. But as
he produced blues artists in the new facility, the emotional side of the

music became foremost for him. Part of his success was his willingness to accept technical mistakes if the result had feeling.

Originally recording local African American talent for other labels, he was inspired to start his own record company after Jackie Brenston and His Delta Cats scored a hit with "Rocket 88." Phillips sold the masters of "Rocket 88" to Leonard Chess at Chess Records. By that time, he had already sold B.B. King and Rosco Gordon recordings to the Bihari brothers' RPM/Modern Records in Los Angeles. Confident in his abilities to find and record area blues acts, Phillips wanted to keep the sales for himself. He felt that he had been cheated out of his royalties on "Rocket 88."

He explained why he founded Sun Records in 1952 in an interview with music writer and historian Peter Guralnick forty years later: "I certainly wasn't even gonna think about the idea of a record label. Then Leonard Chess heard about me, and I played him 'Rocket 88' and it blew his mind. He put that out by Jackie Brenston and Ike Turner. And it was the biggest record far and away that he'd ever had. We sold five hundred thousand . . . that's the equivalent today of probably ten million damn records.

"And even though [Brenston] was black, it wasn't rhythm and blues and it wasn't rock and roll, 'cause there wasn't such a thing.

"It was a shake-hand deal. They were so excited about the record. Leonard was going to get it out. Now this is my version, Leonard's dead and can't defend himself. So I don't usually like to talk about these things.

"I did not want to go in the record business. But I saw that it was going to become totally necessary if I was going to pursue this. Because when you cheat me out of one damn dollar, you have got a problem. And we will not work together. I felt that I had been cheated."[2]

In Sun Records' early years, Sam Phillips discovered and produced important music by an array of bluesmen, including Howlin' Wolf (aka Chester Burnett), Rufus Thomas, Little Milton (aka James Milton Campbell), James Cotton, Ike Turner, Junior Parker, and many others. If his career had ended with his blues recordings, he would still be considered one of the most significant record producers of the last century.

Fortunately, Phillips's career did not end with his blues recordings.

★

In 1996, I traveled from Memphis to Chicago with Sam Phillips, his longtime companion Sally Wilbourn, and his youngest son, Jerry, for the city's blues festival. When we arrived at the Chicago airport, a couple of men were waiting to drive us to the hotel in a large white sixteen-passenger van.

The Chicago Blues Festival is the largest of its kind and claims attendance of a half a million over its four-day schedule. Situated at the Petrillo Music Shell in Grant Park, it is a free event, so no official count is done.

As the executive director of the Blues Foundation, I was to present the Howlin' Wolf Award onstage to Sam Phillips, the man who discovered the award's namesake. We planned to spend the entire weekend in Chicago at the festival.

On the ride to the hotel, I pressed Sam to tell me about some of his remarkable encounters during his career. Although I had known Phillips and his sons, Knox and Jerry, for many years, I still viewed Sam as an almost mythical figure.

"Did Sleepy John Estes's teeth really come out and fly across the room while you were recording him?" I asked.

Sam politely began to tell me the story about that session for what must have been an untold number of times for him. He didn't seem to mind, but I realized at that point how unfair it would be to subject Sam to my questions for an entire weekend. I switched the subject to baseball, which I knew was dear to his heart.

He loved the sport so much that he ran the sound equipment at the local minor league team's home games in the 1950s. Unfortunately, I knew very little about baseball, but that didn't matter. We didn't talk about Elvis, Sun Records, or any of his accomplishments for the rest of the weekend.

Our relationship changed in Chicago. In his eyes, I became his son Jerry's friend. He became Jerry's dad and not the iconoclastic Sam Phillips. He treated me the way my father would have treated any friend of mine if he were with us on a family trip. Although I was in my forties, Sam refused to let me to pick up a check for any meal or pay for a taxi.

He even bought my then-infant daughter, Emma, a present while we were out walking.

After we returned to Memphis, he was always warm and welcoming to me and my family. Sam Phillips was one of the most influential people in the twentieth century, but—stripped of the veneer of his many accomplishments—ultimately he was just Knox's and Jerry's dad.

★

The story of Elvis Presley has become legend. A poor kid from Memphis managed to convince music producer Sam Phillips to record him. During a break, Elvis began goofing around with a black blues song by Arthur "Big Boy" Crudup called "That's All Right." Rock and roll was invented, and the world would never be the same.

That's the legend. Specific circumstances, which could have only transpired in Memphis, allowed Elvis to become the first rock and roll star.

Presley knew postwar blues songs from the radio and Poplar Tunes, a local record shop. Sam Phillips knew the music from his successful career recording black blues artists. A different producer in another market might have seen what Presley was doing as a waste of time, but Phillips knew the power and financial possibilities of black music.

As a producer, Phillips was very much in charge. He knew what he wanted and worked with musicians until he achieved what he wanted. Guitarist Roland Janes described Phillips as a person who always allowed freedom of experimentation: "He wasn't afraid for a mistake being on a record. I made a mistake on a record. I was shy back then and didn't talk very much, so I said, 'Mr. Phillips, I hit a wrong note on that solo.' He said, 'Don't worry about it, that's the feel I want, no one will ever hear that.'

"He was looking for the overall sound and feel. The little side things, like Elvis forgetting the words and start hiccupping. Sam immediately saw something in that while ninety-nine percent of the people in the business back then would stop the tape, correct it, and make sure he was right on pitch and all that kind of thing. Then there wouldn't have been an Elvis Presley."[3]

Before he recorded a note, Elvis was already an idiosyncratic kid. His hair and clothing were not typical of most nineteen-year-old truck drivers. And he was strikingly good-looking. But Memphis had what he needed to be a success: Sam Phillips and the established record industry.

Phillips dedicated his time and expertise to Elvis's raw talent. Other producers may have regarded Elvis Presley as too unorthodox, his take on blues music as folly. Rather than discourage him, Phillips sought to refine and monetize a white musician playing black music in an authentic fashion. And his knowledge and expertise in black music allowed Presley's playful approach in melding contemporary country with R&B to create a new sound.

Some people believe that Elvis stole black music. But when Phillips told the boy that it was okay to play it, black music stole Elvis. It kidnapped him, leading him away from his future as a truck driver who aspired to be a crooner in the mold of Dean Martin, and established him as the "king of rock and roll."

Memphis was entrenched enough in the blues recording industry to have access to pressing plants, radio programs, and distribution outlets. But unlike Nashville, New York, and other recording centers, it was under the radar enough for this new music to germinate unobstructed by major industry influences.

All of these elements coalesced in Memphis in a tiny studio at 706 Union Avenue on a hot July day in 1954.

★

Phillips's work with Elvis Presley was groundbreaking. It opened the door for other early white rock and roll artists and for Sam to develop a roster of new acts.

In November 1955, Phillips sold Presley's recording contract to RCA Records. The proceeds from RCA allowed him to expand the label. By the time he retired from producing to concentrate on his other business interests, Sam had signed or produced a staggering array of talent: Jerry Lee Lewis, Carl Perkins, Johnny Cash, Roy Orbison, Charlie Rich, Warren Smith, Billy Lee Riley, and Sonny Burgess. There were other more obscure artists, but Phillips's success in producing blues and rock acts was unprecedented.

Elvis Presley's early Sun recordings featured a three-piece band with Scotty Moore on electric lead guitar, Bill Black on stand-up bass, and Elvis on acoustic rhythm guitar.

Roland Janes was the guitarist on many of Sam Phillips's rock and roll sessions, including those of Jerry Lee Lewis. He described the transition at Sun between rockabilly and rock and roll during an interview in 1998: "I think our records with Jerry Lee had a lot to do with switching out of rockabilly into rock and roll. Elvis's first records were basically almost a two-piece band. . . . When we came on the scene, Jerry was a little more rambunctious. We had a heavier beat. So we were kinda the transition point from rockabilly into rock and roll. Of course, Elvis picked up the drums and went on with it."[4]

Phillips explained the difference between his early blues recordings and rock and roll: "Rock and roll is the blues with a mania. I mean you take the blues, pull that tempo up, and get that intensity with your instrumentation in addition to singing in an up-tempo.

"And people wonder why that was exciting to young people? Hell, I could be pretty dumb and figure that one out! The one thing people never took into account was the spontaneity of young people. Their response is not as big for anything as it is for music.

"Believe me, the blues is real close to rock and roll. Tempo is the main difference."[5]

★

As he pulled up to the club, he wondered if this was the right place. Paul Burlison was invited to sit in at a small club near 16th Street in West Memphis, Arkansas. It was the early 1950s, and Chester Burnett, aka Howlin' Wolf, invited Burlison, who was white, to jam at his regular Saturday night gig.

They each had radio shows on KWEM in West Memphis. At the time, musicians played short sets of live music interspersed with sponsor messages. Wolf's show followed Burlison's, and they became friends through their music. Eventually, Burlison began to informally sit in with the future blues legend. Burlison was in his early twenties at the time and would later join brothers Dorsey and Johnny Burnette to form the Rock and Roll Trio.

During our interview in 1998, he recalled the circumstances that led him to the club: " I got to telling him, 'I'd like to listen to some of y'all's stuff on the weekends.' He said, 'Come on over Saturday night and sit in with us.' I wanted to meet Willie Johnson who was playing guitar with him, so I snuck off one Saturday night and went over there. I went to the side door and rapped on the door. And they let me in.

"I was the only white person in the whole place. I sat down on a chair beside the bandstand, and he played his whole set. Two or three songs before the set was over, he called me up. I got up and played. He told the band, 'This the guy been playing with me in the evenings.'

"So I sat in and played three or four songs with him. He took a break and walked me back out to my car and stood right there until I got out of sight."[6]

★

Sam Phillips loved radio. Truthfully, he had a longer career and made more money in radio than he did as a record label owner and producer. But many other people, before and after Sam, owned radio stations. So despite his radio success, he will forever be remembered for his contributions in recording American music.

The first time I went into Sam's historic studio at 706 Union Avenue, it was occupied by a transmission repair shop. In 1976, I was charged with compiling an exhibit on Memphis music for Brooks Memorial Art Gallery. Since there had never been such an exhibition collecting artifacts for display, by necessity I assumed the role of archaeologist and detective.

Jim Dickinson and I joined Sam's older son, Knox, at the studio where the transmission shop owners allowed them storage space. As we entered the recording room, Knox pointed out the irregularly spaced ceiling tiles that had helped create the sound Sam wanted. The studio had not been used for years and was cluttered with car parts and equipment.

The sense of history hit me in the face when I walked into the building. Rufus Thomas, Ike Turner, Elvis Presley, Johnny Cash, Little

Milton Campbell, Jerry Lee Lewis, Carl Perkins, Roy Orbison, Sleepy John Estes, and Howlin' Wolf had all made important recordings there with Sam Phillips. This was years before 706 Union was cleaned up and opened as a museum and occasional recording space.

Certainly, the Phillips family knew their place in history. Fortunately, they saved everything. While compiling the exhibition, I looked for Sun records to display in the giant warehouse behind Select-O-Hits Records, a store owned by Sam's brother Tom.

One afternoon as I was leaving, I tripped over something under a pile of discarded records. It was Sam's first recording console, which had been stored and forgotten in the warehouse. An old RCA radio board, this piece of equipment was used in some of the most influential blues and rock recordings in history. It has since been displayed at the Rock & Roll Hall of Fame in Cleveland, Ohio, and the Memphis Rock 'n' Soul Museum, which was developed by the Smithsonian Institution.

In 1959, Phillips built a new studio in Memphis at 639 Madison Avenue, which expanded his recording capabilities. In 1961, he opened a studio in Nashville and continued developing his music publishing, radio, and recording activities. Sons Knox and Jerry joined his businesses, producing local and nationally prominent artists.

Sam gradually retired from the record business when he sold Sun Records in 1969 to record executive Shelby Singleton. He concentrated on his radio stations until his death on July 30, 2003, at the age of eighty.

★

It was a beautiful sunny afternoon in May 1979. A large stage had been built in a field on the site of the former Church Park Auditorium on Beale Street. The main stage of the third Beale Street Music Festival featured blues, jazz, and rock and roll. A crowd evenly mixed, black and white, stood in front, mostly unaware of who was performing next.

As one of the producers of the festival, my charge was to book and present the main stage acts. Over the years, I had the opportunity to showcase numerous legendary performers, including black musicians (James Cotton, Muddy Waters, Koko Taylor, Rufus Thomas, Furry Lewis, Sleepy John Estes, Billy "The Kid" Emerson, Albert King) and white artists (Charlie Feathers, Ronnie Hawkins, Larry Raspberry, Tracy Nelson, Billy Lee Riley, Sonny Burgess, Jim Dickinson).

But nothing prepared me for Harmonica Frank Floyd.

He strolled up the stairs and walked to the lone chair in center stage, which had been set up for him. Wearing overalls and a cowboy hat, Frank sat down and opened his guitar case. After wiping his brow with a red bandanna, he picked up his guitar, put a harmonica in his mouth like a cigar, and began to play.

His set moved effortlessly through blues, country, and rocking tunes. He told jokes, mimicked various animal sounds, and displayed his prowess on harmonica, which had earned him the stage name Harmonica Frank. He played up to three harmonicas at a time blowing one in his mouth while moving it with his tongue and the other two simultaneously through each nostril. He didn't simply play the same lines on multiple harmonicas; he executed contrapuntal melodies as the three harmonicas danced along divergent lines. Every once in a while, he would smile as he took a breath before he continued with the song.

RICK IVY

Harmonica Frank Floyd at Bartlett High School, Memphis, May 1979

Each time he played the festival, I secured a hotel room for him (nothing above the second floor) for a couple of nights paid by the festival organizers. Usually, Frank wanted to remain in Memphis for a few more days, so he would move into my house for the rest of his stay. He was the only performer I booked every year for the next five years.

I began hosting the Harmonica Frank Floyd Fish Fry at the house on the weekend following the festival. I bought carp, which many consider a throwaway fish, and dug a pit in the backyard. Spending most of his life as a hobo, Frank had often slept outside in camps with other homeless men, picking up discarded carp from the riverbanks. He acquired a taste for it and liked the fish cooked over an open flame, the hobo way. So the carp and the pit were especially for Frank.

Harmonica Frank Floyd by the Mississippi River May, 1979

Harmonica Frank Floyd was the missing link between blues and rock and roll. He played blues and country music beginning in the 1920s when he first worked on carnivals and medicine shows. By the time Sam Phillips recorded him in 1951, he was forty-three years old, his lifestyle and music fully formed. Although there were other white musicians playing blues as early as the 1920s, Frank moved effortlessly between country and blues.

If Sam Phillips had been looking for a white man who could play black music in an authentic style, he had found one three years before: Elvis Presley. Frank's recording of "Rockin' Chair Daddy" for Phillips's Sun Records is a precursor of rock and roll. But Harmonica Frank was too old, not attractive and lived the life of a hobo. Phillips found the right formula when he recorded Elvis, who was young, charismatic, and good looking. Despite many musical antecedents, it took those qualities to usher in rock and roll.

When I began bringing Floyd to Memphis for the festival in 1979, he was already seventy years old and living near Cincinnati, Ohio. It was a twenty-hour bus trip, and each year I offered to give him an airplane ticket. He always refused and insisted I send a bus voucher instead. Finally, toward the end of his life (he died at age seventy-five), I tried another approach.

"You know, Frank, when your time comes, it comes. There's nothing you can do about that," I reasoned.

He replied, "I know. But what if it's the pilot's time?"

CHAPTER FOURTEEN

RADIO AND TELEVISION

"I got a couple of record thieves come down here from New York. But they don't know Leonard Chess got here last week and cleaned out the town."
                        —Daddy-O-Dewey Phillips, radio personality

★

Beginning in the 1920s, radio was a major form of family entertainment and a prevalent method of promoting records as music's dissemination changed from sheet music to discs. Radio stations used music recordings as a popular and inexpensive programming alternative to serials and live performances.

In the late 1940s, the *Grand Ole Opry* on WSM in Nashville, Tennessee, and the *Louisiana Hayride* on KWKH in Shreveport, Louisiana, were two live country music radio programs that targeted the same geographic area with their 50,000-watt signals. With the addition of another 50,000-watt station, WLS in Chicago, which also played recorded music, a large portion of the middle of the United States and into Canada was covered.

Four disc jockeys—Gene Nobles, John Richbourg (aka John R), Bill "Hoss" Allen, and Herman Grizzard—played blues on WLAC in the evenings beginning in the late 1940s and continuing until the 1970s.

In 1960, WLS switched its format to Top 40 featuring popular music, including rock and roll. Both stations drew a national audience of young white kids interested in blues-based music.

Cleveland DJ Alan Freed helped bring black music and nascent rock and roll into the mainstream and allegedly coined the phrase "rock and roll." Wolfman Jack, a young fan of Freed, began broadcasting on XERF, a 250,000-watt station based in Mexico that could be heard throughout North America.

As television became affordable in the 1950s and spread across the country, music was still primarily promoted on the radio, although some TV programs featured performances of popular songs. Beginning in 1948, *New York Daily News* columnist Ed Sullivan's Sunday evening variety program on CBS television often featured contemporary musical acts, including Elvis Presley and The Beatles. Steve Allen occasionally hosted rock artists on his namesake show, which was designed in 1956 to compete with Sullivan's telecast.

Ted Mack's *Original Amateur Hour* was a talent competition that included rock acts in a mix of contestants ranging from jugglers to dancers to ventriloquists. Local Memphis artists like the Rock and Roll Trio and The Gentrys both made their earliest national television appearances on the show, which ran from 1948 to 1970 at various times on three networks, NBC, ABC, and CBS.

Based in Philadelphia, Dick Clark's *American Bandstand*, an hour-long television program shown nationally on the ABC network, was considered the most influential. In 1957, after several years of changing sets, hosts, and formats, Clark established the template of teens dancing while singers lip-synched to R&B or rock and roll records.

Throughout the 1950s and 1960s, popular music on television and radio grew into a major method of promoting records. Live performances, jukebox plays, and music journalism were other components of making a hit record.

★

It was almost midnight when two men climbed the stairs to the mezzanine at the Hotel Chisca in downtown Memphis. Longtime veterans of the music business, they were partners in Atlantic Records, one of the most successful independent R&B labels in the country. They had been to town several times over the years promoting their releases and just hanging out with Sam Phillips and Joe Cuoghi, a co-owner of the Poplar Tunes record shop.

When they got to the mezzanine, they saw the broadcast booth where Daddy-O-Dewey Phillips held court. A large glass window separated him from the crowd of teenagers who regularly came to see him at work. His room was small with a few chairs, a couple of turntables, and stacks of records. Its console was situated to allow him to look through the glass window and interact with the kids outside.

As the most popular disc jockey in Memphis, Phillips didn't just play records on the radio. He played the radio for his audience, wisecracking over records, dedications, and live sponsor announcements. Speaking in a fast singsong patter, he was often misunderstood by his conservative bosses at WHBQ, allowing him to say outrageous things. Disc jockeys at that time had the freedom to play whatever music they chose within certain restrictions. Phillips exposed a generation of teenaged Memphians to blues, gospel, and rock and roll.

When Sam Phillips (no relation) recorded Elvis Presley for the first time in 1954, he brought the disc straight to Dewey, who played it over and over. Then he famously located the young singer and brought him into the studio for Presley's first interview. It was Sam who recommended the two salesmen from New York go to WHBQ to see the DJ.

As the two partners, Jerry Wexler and Ahmet Ertegun, reached the booth, Phillips waved them in. Wexler remembered the meeting during our interview in 1980: "We brought some records because that's what we used to do. We used to go around. There weren't that many disc jockeys to worry about. There'll be one or two or three in every town, and there will be one to two or three towns in every state. You make the trip. You see the disc jockeys and bring the new records along."[1]

What they didn't know at the time was that Phillips knew they were coming and was ready for them.

"Ahmet and I came down and he said, 'Stay over there, boy. You get over there.' And then he started doing his thing on the radio. Opening and closing the mike without us knowing it.

"He would say, 'Motherfucker this and motherfucker that.' But he never missed the beat. He would always be cursing with the mike closed. 'All you motherfuckers out there.' There were all these young teenage girls waiting outside. The pimply acne crowd and he was putting us on.

"And then he said, 'I got a couple of record thieves come down here from New York. But they don't know Leonard Chess [owner of rival Chess Records] got here last week and cleaned out the town.'

"After his shift was over, the three of us went out for beers. After a few, Ertegun, a dapper Turkish dilettante, turned to Phillips and said, 'You are a friend of Leonard Chess's, right?'

"Dewey said, 'Oh, yeah.'

"'Does Leonard ever sing you any of his records?' asked Ahmet.

"Dewey said, 'What do you mean?'

"'Does he ever sing you any of his records?'

"'No,' replied Daddy-O-Dewey.

"Ahmet said, 'Well, I could sing you any of mine. In fact, I'll sing you one of Leonard's records.'

"Ertegun sang 'Hoochie Coochie Man' from beginning to the end. Dewey fell off the stool laughing at this son of the Turkish ambassador to the United States singing a Muddy Waters blues."[2]

★

Despite the increasing popularity of black music on national television and clear channel AM radio stations that could be heard at night throughout large areas of the United States, regionalism in music continued into the 1970s. *Billboard* magazine included charts based on sales reported by so-called reporters at retail outlets, but there was no way to verify those numbers.

Before satellite radio was introduced, broadcast frequencies were basically divided into AM or FM stations. Most popular radio stations before the early 1970s were on AM radio, playing a mix of local and national songs.

Record labels were consolidating into a few large corporations referred to as "major," as opposed to independent. Major labels controlled their own production, manufacturing, distribution, and marketing. Independents often relied on a patchwork of manufacturers, distributors, and usually handled their own marketing.

A collaborative relationship developed between major and independent labels. Independents were generally more adept at identifying talent while the major labels could develop and better monetize the artists. Jerry Wexler told me that if a record sold 10,000 copies regionally, Atlantic Records would make a deal to buy the master recording or distribute it nationally.

In the 1950s, the long-playing (LP) record entered the market full-steam; this format allowed more than twenty minutes of continuous music on each side. Record companies began releasing stereo versions of LPs in the late 1950s, and it became the predominant format by the end of the 1960s. LPs allowed artists to increase from two songs under four minutes on one 45 rpm to as many as fourteen on an album.

The new format gave musicians more artistic freedom to expand solos or create thematic works, such as the rock opera *Tommy* by The Who. Longer tunes up to fifteen or twenty minutes required fans to buy LPs to get the music.

AM radio broadcast monaurally while contemporary FM radio broadcast typically in stereo. New programing broadcast in stereo and featuring longer recordings developed on FM radio frequencies. Sensing a trend, broadcast investors began acquiring FM bandwidths. Although music programming continued on AM, an audience shift to FM was inevitable.

The record industry was growing, and FM radio became an important component of that success by the 1970s. It was a boon to the industry, freeing artists from the labels' constraint of including shorter, single songs for AM while offering companies an opportunity to promote full LPs to record-hungry buyers.

The role of the disc jockey evolved with these changes. On AM stations, DJs were typically personality driven and, like Daddy-O-Dewey Phillips, often part of the show. With longer songs, radio personalities had less airtime, becoming more like a friend playing new music for you. And critically, like their AM predecessors, they were able to determine what records were played on their shows. In an industry expanding in size but shrinking in the number of major labels, FM DJs wielded considerable influence over LP sales.

Their status decreased later in the decade with the advent of radio formatting. A consulting firm named Burkhart/Abrams introduced the idea by creating the Album Oriented Rock (AOR) format. As stations signed up to be part of the format, a centrally based music director approved songs.

With radio formatting, disc jockeys no longer had the freedom to air regional or local artists on popular radio stations. Instead, major record labels just had to convince one programmer, the music director, to play their record instead of several DJs in every market. Independent labels seldom had the budget to promote a record in the multiple markets needed to capture the music director's attention.

Radio formatting gave major corporations the ability to control the music being heard. It eventually resulted in a dramatic decline in regional music, a shift that changed the American record industry forever.

★

From the late 1940s until the 1970s, radio was as innovative as its music. Memphis was ripe for a group of pioneers to create a unique sound over the airwaves.

As local music thrived, Memphis radio and television shows featured a mix of regional and national hits. Memphians listened to the *Grand Ole Opry* on WSM, John R. and his cohosts on WLAC, the blues on Chicago's WLS, and Alan Freed on New York's WINS or Wolfman Jack on Mexico's XERF. But their choices were enhanced by several ground-breaking local radio stations.

In 1947, WDIA radio began broadcasting a schedule of light classical, pop, and country and western music. After a year of limited success, white entrepreneur owners John Pepper and Bert Ferguson decided to try something new. They hired local black teacher Nat D. Williams to host *Tan Town Jubilee*, a show devoted to music for a black audience. It was the first such program in the nation.

Similar shows followed. In 1949, the station became the first in the country with black disc jockeys playing music for an African American audience. Although the on-air talent was black, white engineers initially ran the equipment. Referred to as "the mother station of Negroes," it quickly became the number-one station in the market, the center for black culture and lifestyle in Memphis.

WDIA sponsored a youth baseball team; the Teen Town Singers with future stars Carla Thomas and Isaac Hayes; and community announcements specific to black Memphians. They raised money for college scholarships through the presentation of two annual shows, the Starlight Revue and the Goodwill Revue. The office staff was integrated in 1950. In 1954, power increased to 50,000 watts allowing the station to reach nearly 10 percent of the black population in the U.S. The station also had a large audience of young, hip white Memphians.

Rufus Thomas, a black DJ, began working at WDIA in 1951. He described the conditions decades later in an interview with Pete Daniel: "We weren't permitted to turn the knobs or push the switches. We worked on the side of a big plate-glass window. We sat at a table and did the commercials from there. There was a white fellow sitting at the controls.

COURTESY OF MARY ANN AQUADRO

WDIA GOODWILL REVUE '72

NAT D. WILLIAMS

A TRIBUTE TO NAT D.
"The South's FIRST Black Disc Jockey"

SMITHSONIAN INSTITUTION ARCHIVES, ACCESSION 11-009, IMAGE #92-12828 #8A, PHOTO BY PETE DANIEL

ABOVE: Rufus Thomas at the Old Daisy Theater on Beale Street, August 1992

LEFT: Radio station WDIA's Goodwill Revue program from 1972

"We would give him cues, whether to fade or whether to go up and that sort of thing. But in the meantime, I said, 'I am not going to sit here and all of this is going on and I don't know anything about it.'

"So we had a sane-thinking white boy running the knobs. During the day, everybody's there, so he couldn't teach me. But at night, occasionally, his girlfriend would come out there and he would disappear. And when he'd disappear, I would go there twisting them knobs.

"I said, 'I'm gonna learn this, because the time is gonna come that we gonna have to do this.'"[3]

Nat D. Williams, Rufus Thomas, and all the pioneers at WDIA opened the door for the urban format, which has become a major force in contemporary radio. In the process, they delivered regional music and culture to black Memphians and exposed white youth to music they were hungry for.

It was another bridge between the races.

★

Sam Phillips's love of radio was a lifelong passion. He began his career in a small station in his hometown of Florence, Alabama. After achieving success in the record business, he created one of the most groundbreaking station concepts in broadcast history. Fellow Memphian Kemmons Wilson, founder of the Holiday Inn chain of motels, provided financing for Phillips's bold idea.

WHER radio was launched on October 29, 1955. Phillips completed his sale of Elvis Presley's recording contract to RCA Records three weeks later. Ironically, the man who revolutionized youth music in America founded a radio station that only played love songs. At the station, everyone was female from station manager to the sales representatives to the on-air talent, who usually had the responsibility for making sales calls in addition to programming their shows. WHER was on the air in Memphis for eleven years. Disc jockeys were called jockettes, and the decor of the station was decidedly feminine.

"This is WHER, and now the news from a broad," said former on-air personality Betty Berger with a laugh. "I think that's when some listener ran his car up the telephone pole.

"You always knew by the way girls programmed their shows how their love life was going. If everything was happy, you played the happy love songs, like 'Guess Who I Saw Today.' The romantic love songs, that's the only kind of music we played. If you were fighting or having an argument, you would play a little blues love song. So all the girls knew how your affair was going. You didn't have to tell each other about it. You programmed your music."[4]

Sam Phillips's wife, Becky, was a jockette with the station from the beginning. "The plan for WHER was started when Sam was a very young man. One of his main dreams was to own a radio station. And there weren't many women in radio at that time. It was just an idea that Sam thought would work because he liked women in radio. I had been in radio."[5]

Becky Phillips made everyone around her comfortable. She was an impeccably dressed, beautiful woman who was quiet and reserved. Becky opened her home to early rock artists like Jerry Lee Lewis and Johnny Cash, often cooking for them when they came by. Her older son, Knox, told me that when he and his brother, Jerry, were young, she would sometimes wake them after midnight if Elvis dropped by for one of his nocturnal visits.

She had been married to Sam for over fifty-five years when we spoke in 1999, and although they had lived separately since 1968, she still talked about him as her champion. "He just thought that there should be more opportunity for women in radio. Just like he gave black artists a chance, he wanted to give women a chance to bring their talent to the forefront, too. Of course, it was very exciting to me because what I was most interested in, as far as work, was announcing on the radio.

"Because WHER was big-time radio here in Memphis. When it first came on, it was kind of a novelty. But it became much more than that. It was a big challenge, and I think the girls met that challenge and wanted to succeed at something that had never been done by women before."[6]

★

In 1945, there were fewer than 10,000 televisions in U.S. households. In 1950, the number rose to six million, which was 4 percent of households, and reached sixty million or one-third of American homes by 1960. While music heard on TV was not the primary factor motivating record sales, it was becoming an ancillary promotional outlet to radio and jukeboxes.

Daddy-O-Dewey Phillips was the hottest air personality on WHBQ radio when on August 25, 1956, he debuted *Phillips and His Phriends* on WHBQ television. It was shown on Saturday evening at eight; the station executives wanted to bring his young audience to their TVs. The experiment lasted a few months, and on New Year's Eve, 1956, he was given a program called *Pop Shop*, which aired from 3:30 to 4:40 p.m. and was also broadcast on WHBQ radio. A set was built to resemble his radio booth, and Phillips would play records there, mixed with his usual banter.

Pop Shop remained an afternoon staple until January 9, 1958. Replaced by Dick Clark's *American Bandstand*, it moved to 11:30 p.m. and was renamed *Night Beat*. Dewey was joined by Harry Fritzius, an art student, whose role seemed to be wandering around in a gorilla mask. For three episodes, Dewey and Fritzius continued their manic style and outrageous antics until Fritzius went too far one night, and *Night Beat* was canceled. According to *Night Beat*'s director Durrell Durham, Fritzius pinched a promotional cardboard standup of actress Jayne Mansfield on her rear end. He then turned away from the camera and unzipped his pants and tucked in his shirt. By contemporary standards that seems quite mild, but it was scandalous enough in 1958 to have the station cancel the show after just three nights.

Later that year, Dewey Phillips's drinking and drug use led WHBQ to fire him.[7]

★

WHBQ was determined to capture a youth audience for its television station. They hired a more restrained host, Wink Martindale, for *Teenage Dance Party*, a Saturday afternoon program on WHBQ television. While Daddy-O-Dewey Phillips was the nighttime disc jockey on WHBQ radio, Wink Martindale was the much more telegenic morning DJ. After a few years, Martindale left for a career as a game show host in Los Angeles. *Teenage Dance Party* floundered for a few more years with different hosts; in 1964, the station hired George Klein, a fixture in regional radio, for the job.

At that point, Dewey had been off the air for six years, and Elvis was in Hollywood making movies. The Beatles led the British Invasion into America's popular music in 1964, and Klein positioned himself to benefit from this growing interest in English rock music. George kept *Talent Party* on the air for twelve years from 1964 to 1976, becoming a staple in Memphis teenagers' obsession with music. He managed to keep the music created locally on an equal footing with the British Invasion.

"They were trying to save the TV show but wasn't nothing happening. So I auditioned and got the show," Klein recalled. "It was called *George Klein's Talent Party*. I went to them said, 'Look, this is crazy. Just playing records and talking and doing interviews. Let me bring some talent in. It's called *Talent Party*.' And they said okay.

"It was right as The Beatles were hitting. Having been a hot jock, I knew a lot of the acts. I'd call Billy Lee Riley and say, 'I need you to come do the show this week.' I would have six, seven, eight acts come and lip-synch their records.

"Sam Phillips had four, five acts. I could get Jerry Lee Lewis, Billy Lee [Riley], and Roy Orbison. Willie Mitchell had a few acts, including himself and the Bill Black's Combo. I was one of the first TV shows I think Otis Redding ever did. I got a lot of the Stax acts. I was lucky that Memphis was beginning to happen as a recording center and I could get this talent."[8]

★

Music was changing worldwide in the 1950s and 1960s and it was led by events occurring in Memphis. Young residents with an interest in music found their broadcast outlet whether in the late 1940s with WDIA's influential all-black station, Daddy-O-Dewey Phillips's manic radio program, WHER's all-woman format in the 1950s, or George Klein's popular television show in the 1960s and 1970s.

CHAPTER FIFTEEN

JOE CUOGHI AND JOHN NOVARESE

"It wasn't a black and white issue. It was a music issue."
—John Novarese, Poplar Tunes partner

★

World War II ended and its victors came home with a sense of patriotism and optimism, elated at having defeated the greatest threat to civiliza tion in modern times. The Servicemen's Readjustment Act of 1944, also known as the GI Bill, provided low-interest loans, paid tuition for trade schools, and gave other benefits to returning soldiers.

A pair of friends released in 1946 came home and started a business with the help of the GI Bill. Joe Cuoghi and John Novarese had known each other in high school. They grew up as part of the Italian American community that had a strong presence in Memphis. Both of their parents were Italian immigrants who owned neighborhood grocery stores.

"We both got home around March, and everybody had that dream they called fifty-two/twenty. What that meant was the government is gonna pay you twenty dollars a week for fifty-two weeks," according to John Novarese. "Of course, we thought, 'Well, we've got nothing to worry about now.'

"But here's the deal. You sign up and they interview you and they asked about what abilities you have and what have you done in the past.

Then they start sending you checks. But before we got our first one, they found us a job. So we started looking for something to do on our own."[1]

The young veterans decided to try their hand in the food services industry and bought containers of bananas from New Orleans. A friend who owned a fruit stand bought the bananas for a few months until one container arrived filled with tarantulas. That experience ended their involvement in the wholesale fruit business.

"And then we saw the shop [Shirley's Poplar Tunes] for sale one night in the paper," Novarese continued. "We came by the next day and bought it. In fact, we closed the deal on July 12, 1946."[2]

Those tarantulas forced the two into a business relationship that altered the path of music in Memphis. Poplar Tunes, named for its location on Poplar Avenue, remained open for seventy-five years, past the deaths of Cuoghi and Novarese. They were natural entrepreneurs who recognized the financial opportunity in promoting and selling music. After the war, the civilian shortage of shellac, which was used by the military, ended and that allowed more records which included shellac as a component to be manufactured. The euphoria of large numbers of young people returning from war coupled with the popularity of swing music created an uptick in the music business.

The store became a success almost from the time they bought it, in part because of their visionary marketing. At the time, most records were sold in department stores, which closed at 5:00 p.m. Cuoghi and Novarese kept Poplar Tunes open until 9:00 p.m., allowing patrons to shop in the evenings after work.

They became friends with George Sammons who sold and serviced jukeboxes throughout the region. The relationship was fortuitous because Sammons depended on the store to get records for his customers. Cuoghi and Novarese helped Sammons select the most popular titles, and Poplar Tunes found a new outlet for sales through Sammons's jukeboxes. Since most of Sammons's boxes were placed in bars and restaurants, his clients depended on him to place songs that patrons would play. Local disc jockeys would come to the store to hear the latest songs and take advantage of Cuoghi's ability to identify hits.

As jukeboxes became a force in promoting music in the late 1940s, there was a proliferation of new operators in addition to Sammons.

Competition was cordial as several of these new entrepreneurs recognized the need for cooperation. Robert "Buster" Williams and his partner, Clarence Camp, founded a record distributorship in 1945 called Music Sales based in Memphis and New Orleans. They had initially distributed Wurlitzer jukeboxes to operators in the region, shortly before Cuoghi and Novarese bought Poplar Tunes.

In 1949, Williams opened a record manufacturing business called Plastic Products, which pressed records for several labels nationally out of a series of Quonset huts. He also pressed and distributed several important regional labels through Plastic Products and Music City.[3]

Poplar Tunes sold all titles regardless of label affiliation to jukebox operators and smaller retail outlets, while Williams's Music City became a distributor for specific independent record companies. Poplar Tunes was a "One Stop": thanks to its wholesale business, Cuoghi and Novarese could negotiate a much lower price from the labels because of its high sales volume. Many new record stores were in smaller towns throughout the region where labels were unable to send a salesperson. Both Buster Williams's Music City and Poplar Tunes sold these shops records at a wholesale price that still allowed them profitability.

Almost from the beginning, Cuoghi and Novarese created a chart of records they expected to be the top sales and jukebox plays. With their influence on disc jockeys (including Daddy-O-Dewey Phillips), a network of jukebox outlets, and their retail, the charts were often self-fulfilling.

By 1950, Poplar Tunes was a powerhouse in the music industry. The partners were rumored to hold listening sessions after the store closed with influential DJs, like Dewey Phillips and Bob Neal, and label owners, including Sam Phillips, Ahmet Ertegun, and Jerry Wexler. In 1952, Cuoghi and Novarese brought in an employee, Frank Berretta, to manage the retail shop, which allowed them to concentrate on other related projects. Berretta became a partner in the retail store in 1960.

Before his success at Sun Records, Elvis Presley used to come by the store during his lunch break to listen to records. Afterward, he was among the group to hear the latest hits picked by Cuoghi and Novarese, who introduced him to his first manager, DJ Bob Neal. With Neal on board, the two partners gave Elvis his first public showcase at a July 30,

MARY ANN LINDER

DJ Dewey Phillips jokes with Mary Ann Aquadro at Poplar Tunes record shop, Memphis

1954, concert featuring Slim Whitman at the local Overton Park Shell bandstand. Sun had released his first record that month, so Presley was granted the opportunity to be the warm-up act for one of the biggest country music stars of that time.

★

Joe Cuoghi and John Novarese were driven to exploit the burgeoning music scene in Memphis after World War II. In addition to Poplar Tunes, jukeboxes, and the regional network of stores serviced through their One Stop, they promoted concerts. After the success of presenting

Slim Whitman with Elvis Presley in July, they tried a second show in 1954 at the Ellis Auditorium in downtown Memphis.

During my interview with him in 1992, Novarese shared that "Joe Cuoghi brought Piano Red to Memphis at the auditorium on the Bill Haley show. That was never done until that happened here in Memphis. But it went over fantastically. There were no seats available. Bill Haley had a big record then, 'Rock Around the Clock,' but Piano Red has some great records on RCA and people loved 'em. After that, the sale of his records must have doubled. 'Cause a lot of people saw him and liked him."[4]

The chief of police was at the show. The plan was to have Piano Red perform during intermission between Haley's two forty-five-minute sets.

"So I was backstage," Novarese continued, "and Joe says, 'The chief wants to talk to us.'"

"He says, 'You can't go on with this show with Piano Red.'"

"I said, 'Chief, we advertised it! A lot of folks are here for Piano Red.'"

"He said, 'But he's black. You know you can't mix white and black on the same stage.' Piano Red really is black, but he's an albino. So Joe told the chief, 'Chief, do me a favor. He won't go on if you don't want him on, but don't call him black. He's not black and you might hurt his feelings.'"

"'Well, you sure he's not black?' he says.

"He told me to go get him. So I brought him up there and said, 'This is Piano Red.'

"The chief said, 'Oh, well, I didn't know.'

"Once Red started playing, the crowd went crazy. They just loved him."[5]

★

In 1959, the city expanded Poplar Avenue, taking half of Poplar Tunes' space. The three partners built a new store next to the original, which provided more space for the retail and jukebox business. An important component of the new location was the addition of an expansive warehouse, which was the cornerstone of its future success. Originally the warehouse was leased to Record Sales Distributors, but in the late 1960s, it became part of Poplar Tunes.

Poplar Tunes' One Stop shop was already a major force in the regional record business. The charts increased their reach and influence into outlying retail and jukebox locations. Nationally, retail buyers looked at charts in industry trade publications like *Billboard* or *Cashbox* magazines to keep up with best sellers. Poplar Tunes' charts gave them insight into regional releases.

Prior to 1991 when a computerized method of tracking sales called Soundscan was introduced, the national charts were compiled from three sources: radio stations reported the songs played on their stations, retail stores reported sales, and record labels reported wholesale sales. There was no formal verification of the reported numbers.

Poplar Tunes had a symbiotic relationship with the major record labels. Large accounts like Poplar Tunes were allowed 100 percent returns on unsold records and a typically long billing period (sometimes 120-plus days) before money was exchanged. With abundant warehouse space, they could accept large shipments of new releases and store them, winning favor with record labels.

The labels could report huge wholesale sales defined not by payment but by records shipped to retail, which affected the national charts. With Poplar Tunes' charts serving as an important guide to disc jockeys and small outlets, the store had a disproportionate influence on promoting records. If a song became a hit, the store had enough stock in its large warehouse to service their retail, jukebox, and One Stop accounts. If not, they could return all the product to the label for credit, usually before payment was due.

★

Joe Cuoghi and John Novarese focused on expanding their business during the 1950s. They had a network of disc jockeys that helped influence radio and jukebox operators to put records in bars and restaurants. Poplar Tunes was growing in retail and wholesale through the One Stop, and they presented successful live concerts of artists they wanted to promote. Through these efforts, Cuoghi and Novarese could create sales and a regional hit.

In 1952, their friend Sam Phillips started Sun Records and the same year four Los Angeles–based brothers named Bihari opened Meteor Records in Memphis, assigning the oldest brother, Lester, the task of running it. Cuoghi started Hi Records with some Sun Records expatriates in 1957. That same year, a musician named Jim Stewart, who worked at a bank, borrowed money from his sister to found Satellite Records (later renamed Stax Records) in nearby Brunswick, Tennessee. Smaller record labels sprang up throughout the 1950s and 1960s, but these four labels distinguished themselves by owning modern recording equipment and dedicated studios.

Studios owned by independent record labels willing to take a chance on new artists were abundant. Innovative radio coupled with a thriving regional jukebox business created a path to promoting music. And Buster Williams and Poplar Tunes were the last pieces of the puzzle, offering local record pressing, regional distribution, and retail.

By the 1950s, Memphis was like a petri dish where these various elements coalesced into a cohesive community that broke barriers in music. The climate was ripe for the races to reach out to each other and Memphis was one place it happened through a shared musical vision. According to John Novarese, "It wasn't a black and white issue. It was a music issue."[6]

CHAPTER SIXTEEN

HI RECORDS: BIRACIAL RECORDING

"'Do you want to see The Beatles?' 'Do you want to see Ringo?' 'Do you want to see Paul?' 'Well, here's the Bill Black Combo!'... They were throwing stuff on the stage."
—Reggie Young, Bill Black's Combo guitarist

★

In 1935, just a few generations after the Emancipation Proclamation, white Jewish bandleader Benny Goodman integrated his trio by hiring African American pianist Teddy Wilson. There had been a few interracial recordings prior to that, but the Benny Goodman trio was the first publicly interracial group. Hip white audiences had enjoyed black music for years, including informal interracial jam sessions in the 1940s. White Mississippi native Mose Allison claimed to have been snuck into Club Handy in 1949. The inevitably of mixed bands was certain after Goodman had black and white musicians play together in front of an audience.

Several of Sam Phillips's white artists, including Charlie Rich and Charlie Feathers, credited black musicians with teaching them to play blues. There were isolated instances of black musicians on sessions for white artists at Phillips's studio and Lester Bihari's Meteor studio.[1]

When Homer Ray Harris, Quinton Claunch, and Bill Cantrell left Sun Records, they approached Joe Cuoghi for financing. The three had recorded former Sun artist Carl McVoy and lacked the resources to press and release the record. Together with Cuoghi's lawyer Nick Pesce and three other investors, they founded Hi Records and released McVoy's record in 1957.

The release was successful enough to sell out its initial pressing, but Hi Records didn't have enough funding to meet demand, so it eventually sold the master to Sam Phillips. Using that money to convert a former movie house into Royal Studios, Harris and Claunch handled production while Cantrell installed and maintained the equipment.

The plan was to make rockabilly records in the vein of Sun Records. Unfortunately, the early records were unsuccessful, and Cuoghi planned to shut the label down in 1959. Elvis's former bassist Bill Black, who had had a falling-out with Presley, approached his old friend Ray Harris about joining the label as a session musician. While hanging around the studio, Harris, Black, Reggie Young, and a few other musicians recorded the hit instrumentals "Smokie, Pt. 1" and "Smokie, Pt. 2." They named the group Bill Black's Combo to take advantage of Black's association with Elvis. The success of that record persuaded Cuoghi to keep the label active. Royal Studios had mixed sessions almost from the beginning, the "Smokie" sessions among them.

Guitarist Reggie Young described one instance that wasn't racially harmonious: "We were just horsing around in the studio. And I tuned my guitar down and was playing with a pencil, just tapping a shuffle rhythm. Willie Mitchell's piano player, Joe Hall, was the keyboard player. We cut this little old song and called it 'Smokie, Part One' and 'Part Two.' And then the engineer made a racial statement and Joe, the black piano player, heard him say it and walked out of the studio. I forget what the statement was—it was something that was off-color—and Joe got offended and rightly so and left."[2]

★

The summer of 1964, The Beatles began a thirty-day tour of America followed by thirty days in Europe. The warm-up act, selected by the band, was Bill Black's Combo, then led by Bob Tucker due to Bill Black's illness, which cost him his life the next year.

"It was frightening from day one. Because we saw these guys were something else. They were just so popular," Reggie Young said. "There was an hour of music going on before they came on the stage. We opened the show. Then we backed up the other acts, which were The Righteous Brothers, Jackie DeShannon, a group called The Exciters.

"Every disc jockey would come out to start the show and say, 'Do you want to see The Beatles?' or 'Do you want to see Ringo?' 'Do you want to see Paul?' 'Well, here's the Bill Black Combo!'

"Nobody wanted to hear us playing our instrumentals. They were throwing stuff on the stage."[3]

★

When Joe Cuoghi started Hi Records in 1957, he and his partners did not envision that the label would be a soul music juggernaut. Like Jim Stewart's Satellite Records, both labels were established as rock and roll companies in the mold of Sam Phillips's Sun Records. After all, Ray Harris, Quinton Claunch, and Bill Cantrell, three of the original partners in Hi, had worked at Sun. They joined the other investors, which included John Novarese, Cuoghi's Poplar Tunes partner, and their attorney, Nick Pesce.

The recording of "Smokie, Pt. 1" and "Pt. 2" became a much-needed hit for Hi Records after several initial failures. Hi soon established an identity as a country honky-tonk label with a string of successful instrumentals from Bill Black's Combo and their saxophonist Ace Cannon. Although sales were primarily to a white audience, many sessions were integrated.

Over the next few years, black and white musicians found a home at the Hi Records recording facility, Royal Studios. Beginning in the early 1960s, African American trumpeter and bandleader Willie Mitchell became an important component of the developing sound at Hi. Mitchell had one of the most popular R&B bands in Memphis from the 1950s into the 1970s. Always a magnet for talented musicians, his bands in the 1950s included future jazz greats Charles Lloyd and Booker Little.

"Joe was still booking bands and booked Bo Diddley at Clearpool. Bo Diddley got in trouble at St. Louis and didn't show up. He got arrested," according to John Novarese. "The people were completely packed in, and they got a little noisy. Joe went downstairs to a club that had a band led by Willie Mitchell and asked the club owner Bill Norton, 'Let me use Willie tonight to play for the folks upstairs; Bo Diddley didn't show up.' So they made a deal. And after that, Willie came to Hi Records and ran the studio."[4]

With his foot in the door at the studio, Willie Mitchell began developing the sound later made famous with a roster of soul acts. He included African American musicians on Hi Records' honky-tonk releases. The session players at Royal Studios solidified around a mix of white and black musicians. White musicians, guitarist Reggie Young, and keyboardist Bobby Emmons, played with a variety of black instrumentalists, including drummer Howard Grimes, Willie Mitchell, and saxophonist Andrew Love.

Willie Mitchell's gig at Danny's Club in West Memphis ended when the venue closed in 1960 following the Carol Feathers murder. Then he toured regionally but soon established a home base in Memphis at the Manhattan Club, which catered exclusively to whites. During his longstanding engagement there, he generously allowed white musicians to sit in with the band.

Located on the corner of Kerr and Highway 51 South (later renamed Elvis Presley Boulevard), the Manhattan was in the basement of a liquor store. The sale of liquor by the drink was passed in Memphis on November 25, 1969. Prior to that date, patrons could purchase alcohol and bring it into an establishment which would then charge for glasses, mixes (cola, juice, selzer). The synergy between the club and the retail store made the Manhattan Club a destination for white Memphians who were out for an evening.

According to Charles Hodges, patrons could enter either from the liquor store or an outside entrance. Willie Mitchell's group played from 11:00 pm until 3:00 am. Although white musicans were welcome to sit in with black musicians, Mitchell's band had to take their breaks in a small dressing room separate from the white patrons.

"In the studio, we sort of all intermingled," Reggie Young recounts. "As a matter of fact, I played with Willie Mitchell's band with Al Jackson playing drums. This was before Booker T. and all that stuff over at Stax.

Willie was playing at the Manhattan Club down on Bellevue. I used to go over and sit in with them all the time. Joe Hall was the piano player. So we all intermingled there."[5]

By the early 1960s, Hi Records had become synonymous with honky-tonk instrumentals through the continued success of Bill Black's Combo and their saxophonist Ace Cannon, who released hit records under his name. Mitchell was popular enough with white audiences, thanks to his years at Danny's in West Memphis and the Manhattan Club, to release soulful instrumental albums marketed primarily to that demographic.

Elvis Presley merged black and white music at Sun Studio in the 1950s. The next decade, black and white musicians played together at Royal Studios and Stax on a regular basis. By the early 1960s, when Booker T. & the M.G.s became the face of interracial music in Memphis, the races had collaborated in both live performances and the studios.

CHAPTER SEVENTEEN

HI RECORDS: WILLIE STEPS UP

"Just two mikes. But it had a really good impact, just like a heartbeat."

—Willie Mitchell, musician, producer

★

In 1964, Willie Mitchell brought Mabon "Teenie" Hodges, a young guitarist, into his home to groom him for his band. Teenie was one of eleven siblings, including three sets of twins, whose blues musician father had instilled a love of music in him.

Toward the end of that year, two other Hodges brothers joined Willie Mitchell's band, laying the foundation for the Hi Records soul music sound that reached its zenith in the 1970s. Leroy Hodges played bass while brother Charles manned the Hammond B-3 organ. The rest of the rhythm section included drummer Al Jackson or Howard Grimes and Mitchell's step-son Archie Turner on piano.

Within a few years, Mitchell grew his group of young apprentices into a top-notch R&B band, playing on his instrumental records and touring when not playing a steady job at the Manhattan Club. Their tenure at the club was legendary as a location for musicians to drop in and jam.

In 1967, Reggie Young and Bobby Emmons quit Hi Records in a dispute over payments for sessions and joined Chips Moman's studio band at American Sound Studio. Money was tight at Hi Records as sales of honky-tonk instrumentals slowed, although they continued making them for another decade. This opened the door for Willie Mitchell to sign artists and produce more R&B sessions at Royal Studios. He molded the band, which included the Hodges brothers, into a rhythm section he envisioned working in the studio and as his touring unit.

★

Black and white musicians moved freely between Royal Studios and Stax, which was located nearby. As the 1960s were coming to an end, several events changed the dynamics at Hi Records.

Gene "Bowlegs" Miller, a local popular band leader, brought a teenager named Ann Peebles to Willie Mitchell's attention. While visiting Memphis from her home in St. Louis, she asked Miller if she could sing a song with the band. Miller had recorded sessions at Hi and saw an opportunity for his friend Willie Mitchell, who was looking for new talent. Peebles, whose first record was released in 1970, became a staple of the Hi Records soul music roster.

★

The Willie Mitchell band was in demand regionally based on the Hi Records instrumental hits. Popular with show promoters, they would often perform a set of their hits and then provide backing to singers who didn't have their own band.

One day, Mitchell called Charles Hodges with a new booking.

"Hey man, have you heard of this kid Al Green? He got a hot record out called 'Back Up Train.'"

"Yes, I've heard it," Hodges responded. "That's my favorite song."

Willie replied, "Well, he's in Killeen, Texas, says he don't have a band and they want us to come out and back him up. Are you willing?"[1]

The Killeen show was the first on a short trip for the band that changed the fortunes of Hi Records. Willie Mitchell was impressed enough after the gig to offer Green a recording contract. As Al Green

Ann Peebles with Willie
Mitchell at Royal Studios,
Memphis

RICK IVY

made plans to move to Memphis, the band left Texas for their next engagement in Kansas. On the way, they had an accident in their van.

Guitarist Mabon "Teenie" Hodges remembered that moment: "Well, we were on our way to Atchison, Kansas. I'm asleep in the back seat. I hear this explosion and just fall back asleep. I didn't realize the tire had blown out. About ten seconds later, another explosion, so both tires blew out on the front. We turned over twice and ended up in the median. James Mitchell was driving, and he went through the windshield and was about two hundred feet back in the median."[2]

His brother Charles shared, "I remember looking through at the oncoming traffic that was on the turnpike. I could see nothing but tractor trailers and smoke. They locked their brakes because we was rolling over to the other side. When we stopped, we was right up on the edge of it. They called back to Memphis and told them that Willie Mitchell's band was killed."[3]

They played the show that evening despite their injuries. Willie had a broken leg and played sitting on a stool.

Charles continued, "I had just gotten married and it was about two hours before we could call home. Our wives had booked a flight to come claim the bodies. That really stopped us from traveling. We decided then we just wanted to be in the studio. We all agreed, we would come off the road."[3]

The commitment to stay in the studio full time resulted in a string of classic Memphis soul records that solidified their place as one of the greatest producer/rhythm section combinations of all time.

★

Joe Cuoghi died on July 13, 1970, exactly twenty-four years and one day after he and John Novarese purchased Poplar Tunes. That year, Homer Ray Harris resigned as president of Hi Records, selling his shares to Willie Mitchell. Nick Pesce became president and Mitchell became vice president. Although Hi still occasionally released records of Ace Cannon and Bill Black's Combo, Willie now steered the direction of the company.

With his rhythm section in place and brother James leading the horn section, he signed a stable of R&B singers, including Ann Peebles, Al Green, Otis Clay, O.V. Wright, and Syl Johnson. During the 1970s, Willie Mitchell produced a remarkable series of classic soul records at Royal Studios, which were released on Hi Records. He also worked for other labels as an independent producer.

Stax and Hi Records used some of the same musicians on sessions, especially drummer Al Jackson and the horn sections. But each company's records were distinctive and easily identifiable. The differences partly reflect the type of artists Jim Stewart, Al Bell, and Willie Mitchell signed.

Jerry Wexler told Jim Dickinson, "You never know who's the producer in the room. Sometimes it's the guy who brought the coffee."[4] Wexler's point was that producers used a wide variety of methods in the studio. Some directed each musician's performance while others allowed individual session players to interpret their parts on a song.

Every record on both labels was a statement of the artist's vision; the producer's role was to best capture that vision and translate it into a finished product. Certain characteristics of each company's productions shaped the identifying sound associated with their releases. The rhythm sections, studio acoustics, engineers, songwriters, and even equipment all contributed to the distinctive music released by both companies.

The producers molded the sound that became identified with each company. Chips Moman or Jim Stewart produced Stax's earliest records, but Willie Mitchell produced all of the soul albums released on Hi.

As a guitarist, Moman was more involved technically with the musicians. Stewart felt like the music that developed at Stax was a continuation of the black bands from the Plantation Inn and Danny's Club. Stewart was freer with the players and just wanted to capture the overall feel of those bands. Both Stewart and Moman were trying to capture that Memphis R&B sound while bringing studio techniques to enhance it.[5]

Willie Mitchell led the great band at Danny's Club, which was a group the younger musicians listened to as they developed their styles. Chips and Jim may have been members of the audience at Danny's, but Mitchell's perspective was from the bandstand.

Generally, Stax's early records were grittier, punctuated by short bursts by the horns called stabs. They were so prominent that it would be difficult to imagine the Stax sound without horns. Later productions occasionally used string sections, especially on Isaac Hayes or Johnnie Taylor records, and the horns were more integrated into the mix.

The soul records produced by Mitchell used the horns as a subtler component of the sound along with the Hammond B-3 organ, guitar, strings, and background vocals. His brother James Mitchell, a baritone saxophonist, was the arranger and leader of the string section. There was a clearly identifiable Hi Records sound to the soul tracks anchored by the drums.

Willie told me in a 1979 interview how he got the sound on the drums: "Joe Cuoghi told me, 'Willie, you'll never be an engineer. You don't know anything about engineering records, so you go in there and produce the records.'

"So after a whole lot of conversation with him and blowing the roof off and turning cartwheels, I told Joe, 'I can't get the sound I want. I'm going down there and engineer myself.' I said, 'If you don't let me engineer, I'm going somewhere else.' Because my contract had run out with Hi, he said, 'Go on.'

"So I came down to mike the drums and called Al Jackson. I said, 'Al, look man. The drums sound funny. Every time you play, it sounds like a Bill Black or an Ace Cannon record. I think I'll go buy some new drums.'

"So I bought new drums and put the mike on it and it sounded the same way. And I took all the mikes and found a mike that made the bass drum sound like I wanted. Then I put another mike up over the whole kit. And it sounded just like I wanted it. Just two mikes. But it had a really good impact, just like a heartbeat."[6]

★

Al Green had several gold- and platinum-selling albums and singles in the 1970s. In 1976, at the height of his career, he started a church and stopped singing secular songs. Although Hi Records had other moderately successful soul artists—Ann Peebles, Otis Clay, and Syl Johnson—Green's sales were critical for keeping the label profitable.

The next year, the company was sold to Cream Records, a California-based entity.

CHAPTER EIGHTEEN

STAX: THE TORCH IS PASSED

"And to be young and around these seasoned guys was just mind-boggling. It was just—my jaw was open like that."
—Steve Cropper, guitarist, songwriter

★

As the studios crept toward integration in the 1950s, the recent high school graduates frequenting the Plantation Inn and hanging out in the stairwell of Club Handy were coming into their own as musicians. Steve Cropper, Don Nix, Charlie Freemen, Duck Dunn, Wayne Jackson, and Packy Axton were part of the first generation of white Memphians whose careers as professional musicians were integrated experiences.

Various configurations of white kids toured as The Mar-Keys after "Last Night" was recorded in 1961 using black and white musicians from different generations.

"Well, you know a booking agent can't resist booking a job. And so people would call up and say, 'Can you get those Mar-Keys?'" Wayne Jackson explained. "He would call Don Nix and say, 'Don, can you put together some Mar-Keys?' And he would take three or four guys and they would run and make the money. Or he may call Packy who would take a bunch. Maybe it would be Packy and Don together. They just used different guys and go play. They might not even have any horns and go play 'Last Night.'"[1]

While "Last Night" opened some doors for Satellite Records, it closed another one: there was already a record label called Satellite. To avoid legal action, it became Stax, an amalgamation of sibling owners Jim Stewart's and Estelle Axton's last names.

The small independent company was searching for an identity. The country acts who recorded in the former studio in Brunswick had not been successful, while the instrumental "Last Night" sold well in pop and R&B stores. Based on its success, Estelle Axton's son Packy convinced them to record black artists and expand into the African American market.

Chips Moman had been an engineer and producer with Satellite since it began in the Brunswick, Tennessee, studio. In 1960, Jim and Chips converted a former movie theater in a predominantly black Memphis neighborhood into a new studio. The former concession stand turned into a record store run by Estelle Axton.

That year when local WDIA disc jockey Rufus Thomas recorded a few tracks, including one with his teenage daughter Carla, Stax seemed destined to selling to a black audience. Rufus, a popular figure in the black community, had a long history in recorded music, including a hit for Sam Phillips in the early 1950s.

But daughter Carla Thomas's self-penned "Gee Whiz" was the record that propelled the label into R&B prominence, leading Atlantic Records' Jerry Wexler to negotiate a national distribution agreement. The record hit number five on the rhythm and blues chart and number ten on the pop chart, launching her career and Atlantic Records' long-term relationship with Stax.

The plan was for Jim to continue to work at Union Planters National Bank and come to the studio after work. Estelle managed the record shop while Chips Moman ran the studio and produced the early hits. Moman claimed he was promised one-third of the business when he started with the company. Chips quit Stax in 1962 in a dispute about money, and the resulting lawsuit awarded him $3,000. In 1964, he opened American Sound Studio across town and later assembled one of the greatest rhythm sections in history.

SMITHSONIAN INSTITUTION ARCHIVES, ACCESSION 11-009, PHOTO BY PETE DANIEL

Carla Thomas at Memphis
Soundworks Studio, Memphis,
November 1999

★

Steve Cropper had finally realized his dream of playing music professionally. After coming off the road with The Mar-Keys in 1961, he hung
out at the studio learning from the older African American musicians
who had been working in Memphis for years. Pianist Robert Talley, who
in 1960 first told Rufus Thomas about the new studio, served as a mentor
to many of the young white Stax musicians.

Cropper shared some memories with me during our interview in
1999: "It was really good for all of us, the fact that we had so many talented musicians down there. Most of the guys—like Lewie Steinberg,
Floyd Newman, Gilbert Caples—got a lot of their musical knowledge
and training playing when they were in the service in the army bands,
playing jazz and stuff. They already had all these great what we call

'chops' in the business. Musical dexterity, as it were. And to be young and around these seasoned guys was just mind-boggling. It was just— my jaw was open like that."[2]

I had the opportunity to interview Jim Stewart as part of the team for the Smithsonian Institution in 1992. As we sat in the control room of his studio, he offered his perspective on the contributions of the older established musicians playing with the young ones. "The music was a continuation [of Memphis's great black bands] largely. Because what you had with the younger musicians was the influence of Bob Talley," he explained. "These were their peers they learned from, and then they injected some of their own ideas. So it was a combination I think of the old and the new. It was just sort of a gradual process of evolution there.

"I think the younger musicians became more recording technicians, whereas Talley and these people were just good musicians. They were prior to the recording scene, so they never really got involved in the technicalities of the sound and the singer, and playing a certain style or groove depending on the singer.

"Most people know that just about every Stax record was cut with the M.G.s as the rhythm section. You may be able to tell Steve Cropper or Al Jackson, but depending on the artist, it's a little different. Al would play different behind Otis than he would Sam and Dave or Booker T. & the M.G.s because he played for the artist. In the younger musicians, there was that added ability of dealing with that aspect of it. The technicalities and the artist, and the different little inflections and things you'd do depending on who the singer and the artist is."[3]

★

By the summer of 1962, Cropper was established at Stax as a frequent session guitarist. He remembered how he became part of the house band: "We were looking for another good piano player. We had been through several and never found anybody on a regular basis. We were always having to call somebody to play piano.

"Basically, Booker was a horn player. His main instrument was trombone and he played baritone on a couple sessions at Stax. Floyd Newman, our baritone player, suggested that I call Booker T., that he might be the guy to play piano for us. Somebody said that they'd heard him in church and he played organ and piano and he was really, really good. Booker's story was 'I've been playing baritone on some of the sessions. I guess I was stepping on Floyd's gigs. So, he found me something else to do.'"[4]

The quartet of Booker T. Jones, Lewie Steinberg, Al Jackson Jr., and Steve Cropper became the Stax Records' rhythm section. With time left on a session, the guys began jamming on an instrumental, unaware Jim Stewart was recording. When they were summoned into the control room to listen, Stewart was prepared to release the impromptu recording.

"He said, 'If I decided to put this out, have you got anything you can put on the flip side?'" remembered Cropper. "We were just absolutely dumbfounded. Al Jackson, Lewie Steinberg, Booker, and I looked at each other and go, 'Is he serious or what?' We said, 'Well, I don't know. I don't have anything.' And I remembered the riff that Booker had played for me about two weeks ago. I kind of hummed *da, da, da, da*. We go back out in the studio and he started playing this riff and we started playing to it.

"Al started doing a thing and we ran it down in its simple form. After Booker played two verses and sort of turned it over to me, I would do this rhythm: *chink, do, do, chink*. Jim said, 'You know, that's pretty interesting.'"[5]

The B-side instrumental was "Green Onions" and its release necessitated an artist's name. The group was named Booker T. & the M.G.s. As a result, in 1961, one of Memphis's surreptitious interracial recording units was formalized into a working band. "Green Onions" featured Booker T. on the Hammond B-3 organ, an instrument that first became synonymous with the Memphis soul sound in the 1960s.

In Memphis, the B-3 was already part of the jazz sound of Bill Harvey's Band at Club Handy, where Oscar Armstrong was the organist in the 1950s. Lewie Steinberg and Al Jackson probably participated in the jam sessions at Club Handy, while Steve Cropper and his teenaged friends listened from the stairwell.[6]

The sound of the Hammond B-3 organ was also traditionally a part of the church services and early R&B bands in Memphis. Booker T. Jones and his friends made it an integral part of their sound, blending sacred and secular music into a soulful mix. "Green Onions" not only brought an integrated band to the fore but also the Memphis brand of soul music to a wider audience.

Booker T. & the M.G.s included one white member, Steve Cropper, and three black musicians, Booker T. Jones, Al Jackson Jr., and Lewie Steinberg. The band was later evenly mixed, black and white, when Steve's old friend Duck Dunn replaced Lewie Steinberg in 1965.

CHAPTER NINETEEN

THE END OF THE SIXTIES: BIG CHANGES FOR STAX

"I was cold. I was shaking. Then, for a while, nobody was there. They had floated away or drowned. And I felt like I knew I was next."

—Ben Cauley, musician

★

The year 1962 was a momentous one for Steve Cropper and Stax Records. When Chips Moman quit, Steve was promoted to one of the principal producers. After the success of "Green Onions," Booker T. & the M.G.s became the house band playing on most of the records through the remainder of the decade.

Perhaps the most important incident that year was when a young African American singer, who had served as a driver for another act, convinced Cropper to listen to his song. The song was "These Arms of Mine" and the singer was Otis Redding, who became Stax's biggest star until his death in 1967.

During that remarkable five-year period, Redding wrote and recorded a trove of soul classics. He recorded live albums at the Whiskey a Go Go in Los Angeles and in Europe. Redding was introduced to a younger white crowd at the Monterey Pop Festival where he stole the show. The

Grateful Dead's rhythm guitarist Bob Weir said Redding's performance at Monterey was like seeing God on stage.[1]

Recording sessions in Memphis are often collaborative efforts between musicians, singers, and producers. Songs take shape during the course of running through the chords, and arrangements can be malleable usually depending on the particular producer and rhythm section. At Stax, the music often developed while the tape was running.

Duck Dunn described a typical session and how Otis Redding changed things: "It was a complete collaboration. Booker or Isaac or somebody could give me a line to play. And if I strayed from it, and it helped it, they didn't force you to do that. It was just—they gave you your space.

"When [Otis Redding] did 'Respect'—and I never will forget—most of Stax's stuff was done with a lot of whole notes and half notes and stops with the horn section. When he did 'Respect,' and he started that intro, *da-da-da da-da-daa*. They looked at him. They never heard anything like that before. I said, 'Jesus.' I didn't believe it was going to work. Man, it came off. He was just a joy and he always smiled."[2]

Otis was bringing Stax soul music to a much bigger audience when he was killed in an airplane crash along with label mates the Bar-Kays outside Madison, Wisconsin, in December 1967. It was a tragedy that set Stax on its heels. The Bar-Kays, recent high school graduates, had recorded a hit titled "Soul Finger" and had been touring as Redding's backup band. They were just kids, most fresh out of high school. The Bar-Kays had performed in Cleveland, Ohio, on Saturday, December 9, backing Otis Redding on a short weekend run of shows. The private airplane left the next day around noon for that night's show in Madison, Wisconsin.

Their routine was for two members to stay behind and return the rental vehicles, catching a commercial flight to the next engagement. That afternoon, bassist James Alexander and guest vocalist Carl Sims stayed behind. With no available flights to Madison, they flew to Milwaukee where the pilot was to pick them up after dropping off the band.

Trumpeter Ben Cauley sat behind Redding who was in the co-pilot's seat. Phalon Jones sat across from him. It was cold and foggy in

SMITHSONIAN INSTITUTION ARCHIVES, ACCESSION 11-009, PHOTO BY PETE DANIEL

The author with Ben Cauley at Inside Sounds studio, Memphis, December 1999

Madison, and upon the descent, the airplane crashed into Lake Monona. Cauley was the only survivor of the crash and the only one on board who could not swim.

"I was cold, I was shaking," Ben told me. "Then, for a while, nobody was there. They had floated away or drowned. And I felt like I knew I was next. I saw Ronnie [Caldwell] come out. Ronnie came up and he was hollering for help. And I was saying, 'Ronnie, hold on, man. I'm trying to get over to you.'

"I had this airplane seat, man. I was trying to get to him, and the more I tried to get to him, it was slipping out my hand. And finally it slipped out of my hand, and at that point, I said, 'Oh, no.' I knew I was next because I didn't have one, and another one came straight to me."[3] By this time, rescue boats arrived and pulled Cauley out of the lake, and he was told to lie down as others were retrieved from the waters.

Alexander and Simms waited at the airport in Milwaukee for the pilot. When they heard about the accident, they were picked up and driven to Madison. "I was numb," Alexander remembered. "First of all, I was seventeen years old. I had never had any kind of experience like that. But I guess the moment of truth came after they brought us from Milwaukee to Madison, Wisconsin. The authorities came and got us and the first thing that we had to do is go to the morgue and identify people.

"Just a strange thing to do, especially when all these guys in the group were your friends and you grew up with them and stuff like that, and then here you have to go and identify them in a morgue. That's tough."[4]

Stax publicist Deanie Parker, a bright powerhouse in a key role at the label, recalled the days following the accident: "I think that I remember our wondering where do we go from here, because clearly at that time Otis was destined to be the biggest artist. Most important, Otis was a wonderful human being. He was a little bit shy, soft-spoken, fun, genuine. But not only that, we had another group of very, very talented young men who were studying the musicians' every move.

"It was an incredible loss. What we experienced in that place that night when we first heard it. I don't think that any of us who are still living have forgotten where we were at the time we heard the plane had gone down in Lake Monona.

"For days after that, it was horrible. There was a funeral every day it seemed. The search was going on. It was the dead of winter. I think probably the worst experience that I had after it was all over, they delivered those trunks from that plane that had their clothes and things in them. Water was still dripping out of them into the studio. It was just miserable."[5]

Then on April 4, 1968, the Reverend Dr. Martin Luther King Jr. was assassinated at the Lorraine Motel where many Stax artists stayed while in town. It was a turbulent time for Memphis and the nation. The city leaders were rightfully concerned about the reaction of the African American citizens. Stax artist Isaac Hayes was asked to serve as a spokesperson to bring calm to the city.

Deanie Parker continued, "Apparently, people in high places, especially in the political arena, really didn't think very much of what we were doing until they needed someone they thought could appeal to the people who they thought were going to burn this city down. Then Isaac Hayes and Stax Records became very important. That says something about this city and what was going on at that time. Until that time, they probably would not have even wanted anybody to know that we existed. They certainly didn't approve of what was going on at Stax because everything we were doing was very evil."[6]

★

Change was in the air for Memphis music. In 1968, after the assassination of Dr. King, Stax's longtime distribution agreement with Atlantic

Records ended. Jerry Wexler and Ahmet Ertegun had sold their company, Atlantic Records, to Warner Bros. in 1967. The sale triggered a proviso in Stax's distribution agreement: if Wexler was not involved, the contract would terminate. The problem was, according to the Stax contract, Atlantic now owned all of the master recordings it had been distributing. This meant no catalog sales for Stax the year after their best-selling artist died.

Catalog sales are the lifeblood of record companies. They provide cash flow from product that typically has no costs beside distribution, manufacturing, and licensing. The production and marketing expenses were often already recouped during the initial sales period. Artist royalties were usually advanced against sales when the master tapes were accepted, and often the advance was not recouped. This meant that no payments were due to the artist until the record had sold large numbers.

Larger retail outlets often had generous billing periods, sometimes resulting in a full quarter or more before the labels collected on new hit records. Catalog sales were ongoing, and although the billing periods were still stretched out, the longevity of sales gave record labels a steady stream of operating cash while searching for their next hit. The loss of Stax's catalog was potentially devastating to the company.

★

Al Bell joined Stax as a radio promotions specialist in 1965. The company was riding a crest of hit records, including Otis Redding's, and wanted assurances that black radio stations would play their records. An African American former disc jockey, Bell rose through the ranks of the company, serving as vice president and later as co-owner with Jim Stewart and eventually as the sole owner.

Stax was now a fully integrated company from musicians and producers to owners. But they were also a record label with no catalog. Bell oversaw an ambitious effort to release enough product to quickly rebuild. The idea was to get records into the marketplace and build a new catalog.

In late 1968, Stax was sold to Gulf & Western, a large conglomerate looking to diversify its holdings. Estelle Axton left the company in 1969, and Al Bell was promoted to vice president. He knew it was critical for Stax to have more hit records if it was going to survive. During an eight-month period, Bell supervised the release of twenty-seven albums and thirty singles in his plan to restock the catalog. Gulf & Western held the company until 1970, when Jim Stewart and Al Bell bought back the label.

By 1970, both Stax Records and Hi Records, stalwarts of Memphis soul, had African Americans included in ownership, with Willie Mitchell and Al Bell influential in signing artists and shaping the direction of their labels.

CHAPTER TWENTY

AMERICAN AND ARDENT STUDIOS

"They came to get the players. That was the drawing card."
　　　　　　　　　　　　　　—Reggie Young, guitarist

★

After Chips Moman left Stax in 1962, he started American Sound Studio a few years later. Still an in-demand session guitarist, Chips kept his hand in studio work in Memphis, Nashville, and Muscle Shoals, Alabama.

He produced a Memphis teenage band called The Gentrys at American and landed a hit with a song called "Keep On Dancing." Moman continued producing, writing, and playing sessions wherever his clients preferred, while establishing a regular group of musicians used on his recordings.

Guitarist Reggie Young and keyboardist Bobby Emmons both quit Hi Records in 1967 in a dispute over session pay. Moman convinced the two, along with bassist Tommy Cogbill and drummer Gene Chrisman, to form a rhythm section that would record exclusively at his American Sound Studio. According to Young, the conversation with Chips went like this: "Let's don't go to New York or go to Nashville or whatever. If they want to use us, come over here and get us."[1]

The group later expanded to include Mike Leech as an alternate bassist and Bobby Wood on keyboards. Although other producers and engineers worked at American Sound Studio, the musicians hired to form the rhythm section always came from the same group established by Moman.

They backed black and white artists with equal success, although the band included only white musicians. Some of the singers who recorded chart-topping records during those years at American include Neil Diamond, Elvis Presley, Joe Tex, Sandy Posey, Merrilee Rush, Dusty Springfield, B.J. Thomas, Bobby Womack, The Box Tops, and Wilson Pickett.

★

American Sound Studio was renowned as a place labels and producers could take singers and make hit records with their rhythm section. As the studio grew more successful, songwriters were brought in to pitch material to the producers.

Dan Penn and Spooner Oldham were songwriters from nearby Muscle Shoals, Alabama, who became fixtures at American. Penn especially hoped to become a producer and found a young singer in Memphis he wanted to produce. Moman agreed, and in August 1967, the teenager and his band cut a classic Memphis record under Penn's direction. The band was called The Box Tops, with vocalist Alex Chilton, and their first release, "The Letter," became a number-one record in the United States. Penn needed a follow-up hit but was struggling. He enlisted Spooner Oldham to help write a hit song, and the two spent three days without success.

Penn told me the story during our interview in 2000: "So, you know, we got together and stayed together for about three nights. We wrote stuff on paper, we hung, we played cards, we did everything that we always do. And it was just like . . . and we couldn't buy a buzz. You could drink coffee, you could do anything you want to. You were still exactly where you were."

They decided to go across the street to a restaurant called Porky's and have a meal before heading home dejected. "We're in the booth. I'm looking at him, and he's looking at me. And out of the blue, he put his head over on the table and said, 'I could just cry like a baby.' And I said, 'Spooner, what did you say?' He said, 'I could cry like a baby.' It just hit me, just like a big lightning bolt. I said, 'That's it. That's what we're looking for. That's what we've been looking for.' And he looked back at me and it hit him. . . . So we just said, 'Hey, keep the food. We're way past food now.' I just threw him some money, and by the time I was opening the door to the studio, we already had 'When I think about the good love you gave me, I cry like a baby.'"[2]

Inspiration comes from different places. The Box Tops' follow-up hit to "The Letter" was "Cry Like a Baby," which was the number-two song on both the Billboard and Cashbox Hot 100 charts. It sold over a million copies in the United States.

★

During their time at American from 1967 to 1972, the rhythm section was on 120 top-ten records. It was an amazing run, including one week when twenty-five songs on the Billboard Hot 100 chart had all been recorded at Moman's studio with his rhythm section.

"They came to get the players," Reggie Young reflected. "That was the drawing card. Moman started asking points [percentage of sales] and instead of giving them a three-hour session, we was giving them a five-hour session plus points to do records. . . . I think that's what kind of put us out of business, saying we wouldn't cut unless we got a percentage of the record."[3]

In 1972, Moman and the core of the rhythm section moved to Atlanta expecting to continue their success. Bobby Wood had already quit the band, and Tommy Cogbill remained in Memphis.

"We put the studio in and were waiting for the business," Young said. "We thought we could do our own acts and share in a production company and get rich and retire. But that didn't happen."[4]

After less than a year, Moman and the session musicians closed the studio in Atlanta and moved to Nashville where they stopped working as a formal unit. They re-formed for a few shows and occasionally recorded together but never duplicated the level of success they had achieved in Memphis.

★

For a little over a decade beginning in the mid-1960s, Memphis music was booming. Between Chips Moman's parade of hit records for other labels and Hi and Stax churning out hits, the city was the third-largest center for recording in the United States.

Three prep school classmates—John Fry, John King, and Fred Smith—began experimenting in the late 1950s with a studio built in the Fry family's converted garage. They produced and released a few records and concentrated on upgrading equipment for their recordings. All three were interested in improving the sound of existing radio consoles, which were the primary equipment used in small studios. The three friends eventually ended their partnership. John Fry continued to build a career in the studio business at Ardent. John King began working in radio promotions, and Fred Smith founded FedEx, the delivery service based in Memphis.

When the Fry family home was sold, John needed a new space for his studio. In 1966, he rented a building on National Street that became the home of Ardent Studios, the name he and his former partners had chosen. Fry had built much of the equipment used in the garage studio, but by the time he was ready to install the new facility's gear, the state of studio equipment was more sophisticated.

Fry explained how he bought the console for the National Street facility: "Originally, we intended to build a console ourselves. Before we got very far into this, a fellow named Welton Gitane showed up. He came in and introduced himself and said that he was building a console for Stax. He brought in one of the channel strips out of the console. It was entirely solid state. We decided we would build a console based on these channel strips from this company called Auditronics, which was Gitane's firm."[5]

That was a fortuitous decision that helped shape the young studio's future. Gitane built a recording board for Stax and another for a company, co-owned by WDIA founder John Pepper, that produced and recorded radio identifications and jingles. Gitane went to work for Pepper as an engineer. With a new facility and equipment familiar to

Stax and Pepper's company, Ardent was hired to record the overflow business from both.

"We had two early customers that had great influence on me. One of the early customers was Pepper, the jingle company. Once we had gotten our studio built, it was working out well acoustically," Fry explained. "Welton started directing a lot of their overflow work to us. Initially, their engineers would come out and do all of that. What they did was really interesting and uncommon for this part of the country, because they would record large orchestral ensembles.

"They would record big band style—four trumpets, four trombones, four woodwinds, and rhythm section. Sometimes they would use a large string ensemble. I got, at a very early stage, to start engineering some of those sessions. Well, normally, that's the kind of experience that you would not have gotten in this part of the country."[6]

The young engineers at Ardent had the opportunity to record a wide variety of instruments, experimenting with microphones and placement of musicians. It was an education that was rare outside of major recording centers like New York, London, and Los Angeles.

Fry continued his description of those times: "The other early client Welton really introduced us to was Stax, because Welton had built the first real console that Stax had in the McLemore Street studio. And they started sending us a lot of their extra work, and they had more stuff than they could do. And not to be critical, but they didn't have the best environment for mixing. A lot of the producers wanted to do something different. So almost all of their producers were coming over to our place and doing stuff."[7]

In 1971, John Fry opened a new state-of-the-art facility on Madison Avenue. They continued handling the overflow from Stax and generated a client list, including Led Zeppelin, James Taylor, ZZ Top, Leon Russell, Cheap Trick, and Journey.

Fry was generous with his time serving as a mentor to countless engineers. Aspiring recording personnel always began by making coffee and answering the studio door after-hours; they were then sometimes allowed to watch or serve as assistants on sessions with more seasoned personnel. Eventually, the dedicated ones became engineers and producers.

Jim Dickinson and Terry Manning were the first engineers hired for the studio on National Street. They learned the craft with Fry.

Once Ardent moved to its Madison Avenue address, which included two studios, business was brisk and engineers were in demand. John Fry's tutelage shaped a generation of creative talent that established Ardent as a destination for artists seeking the Memphis vibe. In addition to Dickinson and Manning, a partial list of producer/engineers who learned their trade under Fry includes Joe Hardy, Jon Hampton, Jeff Powell, Skidd Mills, Paul Ebersold, Brad Blackwood, Curry Weber, Adam Hill, and Pete Matthews.

Young bands were given the opportunity to record at Ardent often without a label. His cadre of engineers was always on the lookout for talent and could bring them into the studio to rehearse and record. Ardent Records was the entity John Fry used to sign local groups to production agreements. He encouraged creativity and helped foster the careers of Memphis musicians who learned to record without the pressure of outside companies overseeing the process. One of the most successful of these was Big Star, a band that Fry produced in 1971.

He remembered the circumstances during our interview in 1999: "Alex Chilton had been the lead singer in The Box Tops. His deal ran out and he didn't want to make any more Box Tops records. Terry Manning worked with him and made a solo album. Then Alex went off to New York. He was up in New York hanging out with Keith Sykes. Then he came back to Memphis and got involved with a band with a bunch of Memphis folks. One of the guys in there was Chris Bell. Chris was already spending a bunch of time around the studio, and Andy Hummel played in bands with Chris before. Jody Stephens was the drummer. So, Alex, Jody, Andy, and Chris were Big Star."[8]

While critically acclaimed, the first two Big Star records didn't sell. Ardent Records was distributed by Stax, which was distributed by CBS. The arrangement with CBS proved difficult for Stax in many ways.

Chris Bell quit the band after their first record was released in 1972; he died in an automobile accident in 1978. Andy Hummel left the band after the disappointing sales of the first two records. Two more Big Star studio records were made before Alex Chilton died in 2010. Their influence on modern rock music was substantial, and bands like R.E.M., The

Replacements, The Posies, Gin Blossoms, and others each took something from their sound.

In the late 1970s, two Memphians named Eddie DeGarmo and Dana Key began to experiment with rock music tailored to a Christian audience. They came to Ardent and began working with Fry.

"I became a Christian in '78," Fry told me, "and started working with those guys. They didn't have any money. I mean, they gave them tiny little budgets to do these records. So, we'd charge the Christian guys about twenty-five percent of what we charged the pagan guys. Because we wanted to encourage that. We thought that was a good thing to do."[9]

John Fry was a friend and mentor for generations of Memphis musicians, producers, and engineers. He was involved in civic endeavors designed to improve the lives of people in all facets of the music industry. Following his death in 2014, the apprenticeship program at Ardent ended, as the label and studio sought out a new identity under the leadership of his wife, Betty Fry.

CHAPTER TWENTY-ONE

THE END OF STAX, HI, AND AMERICAN

*"I didn't have nothing but candlelights and it was Al Green.
He came in a white suit, black briefcase."*

—Howard Grimes, musician

★

In the 1970s music industry in Memphis, black and white people were
working together in studios and in boardrooms. Jim Stewart and Al Bell
were partners at Stax Records while Nick Pesce and John Novarese were
partners with Willie Mitchell at Hi Records. Memphis was still suffer-
ing after the murder of the Reverend Dr. Martin Luther King Jr. with
strained race relations even among musicians.

When Al Bell bought Estelle Axton's share of the company after the
dissolution of the deal with Gulf & Western, Stax was at a crossroads.
He had signed enough acts and released a new catalog of records to
replace the ones lost to Atlantic Records in 1968 and handled distribution through a series of independent companies.

Johnnie Taylor was considered the next great soul singer after the
death of Otis Redding. The records of longtime Stax producer and session man Isaac Hayes were selling, and songs by The Staple Singers, a
gospel group, were becoming anthems for the civil rights movement. A

new roster of artists was forming, and the company seemed headed in the right direction.

Branching into pop music with a subsidiary label, Enterprise Records, Al Bell signed white rock artists, including Larry Raspberry, who had been the lead singer of The Gentrys. In 1971, Big Star released the first of two critically acclaimed rock records on Ardent Records, then distributed by Stax. Big Star continues to be an influence on popular music and retains a cult status.

The year 1972 represented a turning point for Stax. Isaac Hayes, who recorded the soundtrack for the movie *Shaft* about a black detective, became the first African American to win an Academy Award for Best Original Song for the "Theme from *Shaft*." Encouraged by Hayes's success, Bell decided to expand the Stax brand into films and other media endeavors. That same year, he staged a concert in Los Angeles called Wattstax featuring artists from the roster of the label. Drawing a crowd of 100,000, the concert was filmed for theatrical release. Between Hayes's Oscar-winning soundtrack song for *Shaft* and Wattstax, it seemed like the company was ready to expand into a broader entertainment entity.

Also in 1972, Bell bought Jim Stewart's shares of the company and became the sole owner of Stax. He signed a distribution agreement with CBS Records president Clive Davis, who saw the arrangement as a way for his company to enter the African American marketplace. Unfortunately, Davis was fired a few days later, leaving Stax as an outlier in a corporation that was primarily a rock music label. No one else at CBS shared Al Bell's vision of Stax as a black entertainment company focused on music, movies, and television. With a sales and marketing staff unfamiliar with black music, CBS was not a good situation for Stax in the early 1970s. Ultimately, Clive Davis's firing became a turning point in Stax's story.

★

Willie Mitchell produced definitive soul records for Hi during the 1970s. He always used the Hodges brothers along with other members of his core rhythm section. Al Jackson Jr. and Howard Grimes alternated on drums, depending on who Mitchell thought felt the groove best. His brother James arranged the strings.

Despite classic releases by Ann Peebles, Otis Clay, O.V. Wright, and Syl Johnson, Mitchell's greatest success, artistically and financially, came from his productions with Al Green. During the early and mid-1970s, they broke barriers by landing hits on both the R&B and pop charts. Green was riding a peak in popularity when, in October 1975, Al Jackson Jr. was murdered by an intruder in his home. Green was affected by losing his friend and drummer. "When we had the misfortune of losing Al Jackson, it kind of dampened my spirits because I rode on the rhythmic pattern that he played," said Green in a 1978 interview with me.[1]

On October 18, 1974, Mary Woodson, a woman Green once dated, showed up unexpectedly at his home in Memphis. She burst into his bathroom, poured scalding grits on the singer as he was in the bathtub, and then killed herself in an adjacent bedroom. These events led Al Green to reevaluate his life, become an ordained minister, and open the Full Gospel Tabernacle Church on December 18, 1976.

Reverend Al Green in his conference room, Memphis, December 1978

Music was a centerpiece of Green's sermons. "My ministry has been given to me to preach the gospel of Jesus Christ," he explained. "Music speaks louder than words. . . . And I can reach much more people in singing. So I just sing what I want to say."[2]

As his music changed from sexy soul to gospel, record sales began to slip. In 1977, Hi Records was sold to Los Angeles–based Cream Records and operations were moved to California. Willie Mitchell maintained his ownership of Royal Studios and stayed in Memphis working for Cream/Hi Records and as an independent record producer.

★

As Hi Records was ending its time in Memphis, Stax was experiencing its own demise. Despite a roster of successful artists, including Isaac Hayes, The Staple Singers, and Johnnie Taylor, the label was overextended and struggled with severe cash flow problems.

Al Bell's ambitious attempt to expand into an entertainment entity required a major investment. In the early years of the label, Jim Stewart had worked at Union Planters National Bank during the day until the business generated enough income to support him. That relationship led to the bank becoming a lender to Stax from its inception.

In 1972, when CBS signed the distribution agreement, it appeared that Stax had turned the corner with a new catalog, a roster of hit makers, and a national distribution system in place. Bell took out a loan from Union Planters to finance the company's expansion plans with the working capital needed.

Record companies rely on working capital to finance production, salaries, operating expenses (rent, utilities, etc.), and marketing. Typically, a national distribution agreement included sales, warehousing, and manufacturing. The major companies owned the warehouses and pressing plants, and those costs were charged back to the labels before payments were made for records sold. It was a delicate balancing act that required cash reserves to keep the label afloat. If a record didn't sell, the manufacturing costs of the stock in the warehouse was deducted from titles that were more successful. This was called cross-collateralization, and it was a typical clause in music industry contracts. If the unsold product stayed in the warehouse too long, warehousing fees were added.

In the case of a hit record, the distributor always made sure that manufacturing kept up with demand since their profits were based on units sold. Of course, the manufacturing costs were always an expense to the label. In the instance of a record that seemed like a hit, sometimes retail ordered excess copies to be assured of having stock.

Since the payments often were not due for extended periods and returns were offered at 100 percent, a hit record sometimes generated tremendous manufacturing and warehousing costs, which were held against returns. If the titles didn't sell in enough retail outlets, returns were substantial and labels could lose money on hit records. With cross-collateralization, the losses could carry over into more successful releases and impact the final payments to the record companies.

When Clive Davis was fired as the president of CBS, Al Bell lost his champion. Their handshake deal had called for CBS to pay Stax for every record it delivered, regardless of sales. CBS changed the agreement and cut payments to Stax by 40 percent. Bell accused CBS of pressing too many records and purposely keeping product in the warehouse despite a demand in retail.

As bills poured in and without the benefit of a productive partner in CBS, Stax experienced financial hardships. Union Planters National Bank called for payment of the loans, which forced Stax into bankruptcy and essentially out of business. The company's assets were sold. And validating Bell's claims of bad faith, CBS Records signed several major hit makers from the label.

In late 1975, Stax officially closed. Then in 1977, the post Atlantic Records–distributed catalog was sold to Fantasy Records, a California-based company. Along with the sale of Hi Records in 1977 and the earlier departure of Chips Moman and American Sound Studio, the recording business in Memphis experienced a precipitous fall from which it has yet to recover.

★

One day in 1970, Willie Mitchell was in the control room at Royal Studios sitting with Al Green. The session was about to start. The rhythm section with Charles, Teenie, and Leroy Hodges was in the main tracking room, and Howard Grimes was set up in the drum booth.

Grimes talked about that day during my interview with him in 1999: "'It seemed like everyone was getting rich but me,' I said with the drum microphones on. 'I'm tired of making people rich and I don't have nothing.'

"Then a voice came back from the control room saying, 'There's going to be some changes around here. There's going to be a lot of changes.'

"At that point, the band fell silent. I came out of the drum booth and said, 'Man, who are you talking to?'

"'As a matter of fact, you,' said Al Green. 'You're fired.'

"I responded, 'You can't fire me. I work for Willie Mitchell.'

"Mitchell, hearing all of the disruption, came out of the control room to diffuse the situation. He said, 'Wait a minute, Al. I do the hiring and firing.' A furious superstar, Al Green stormed out of the session. And I never did another session for Al Green."[3]

After Hi Records was sold in 1977, Willie Mitchell gave severance money to his studio musicians who were losing their income. But things grew bleak for Grimes once that money ran out. He became ill and was out of money. His wife left him, and he eventually lost his home, living on the street for more than three years.

Grimes described an incident that occurred during this time: "Before I lost my home, my utilities and everything was turned off. It was in the wintertime. And I had nothing but a Bible that was given to me. . . . One night, it stormed real bad and I heard a knock at the door. I didn't have nothing but candlelights and it was Al Green. He came in a white suit, black briefcase. Al gave me five hundred dollars. I hadn't seen no money in over two months. He was kind of leery about being out in the storm. But when he saw me, he had this wonderful smile on his face. I was afraid to take the money.

"He said, 'I've never been out in a storm for nobody. But everything will be all right for you. Take this money.' He laid the money on the table and said, 'You go tomorrow and have your utilities and things turned on.'

"I was afraid to take the money, because there was no way I could pay him back. I never would have thought that he would be the one who came to me, and then he gave me an opportunity to come to his church."[4]

Eventually, Grimes recovered from homelessness and began to work again as a session drummer. He occasionally found work with the Hodges brothers in a group called the Hi Rhythm Section.

But there were more tough times coming for Memphis music in general.

CHAPTER TWENTY-TWO

A NEW PARADIGM

*"That's all well and good, and I'm sure my wife would love
that, but I can't spend taxpayer funds for that."*
—J. Wyeth Chandler, mayor of Memphis (1972–82)

★

In 1973, sales of U.S. recorded music were $2 billion and rose each year
until 1978, when record revenue reached $4 billion annually. A decline
began in 1979 with sales not recovering back to 1973 levels for more than
a decade.[1]

The 1970s are critical years in the story of Memphis music. In 1972,
the year Stax signed its disastrous contract with CBS, Chips Moman
moved his studio out of town. By 1975, Stax was bankrupt and its assets
sold. Hi Records, sold in 1977, moved to California. Musicians, engineers, and producers scrambled to find work, often leaving for either
Nashville or Los Angeles.

There were many factors in the decline in record sales in the late 1970s.
The blockbuster *Saturday Night Fever* (1977), a film that featured dance
as a centerpiece of the narrative, was largely set against the backdrop of a
fictional discotheque in New York. The musical style associated with the
film came to be known as disco. Discotheques had been around since the
1960s in New York and other urban areas, but it was *Saturday Night Fever*

that brought the music to a mainstream audience. Disco was intended for dancing, not listening, resulting in a loss in record sales. Fans who had passionately collected jazz, rock, or soul albums and tapes were replaced by an audience more interested in practicing dance moves in groups at the clubs. As disco music became ubiquitous in 1979, sales dropped and had a slow recovery back to earlier levels.

The structure of the music business was also changing on a global scale during this decade. Seemingly unrelated events led to a new paradigm in the industry.

During the free-spending years in the 1970s, major record companies had regional offices with sales people covering their territories by driving from stop to stop. Although the offices were usually only staffed by a few people, many labels had offices in New York, Philadelphia, Atlanta, Miami, Memphis, Dallas, Detroit, Chicago, and other key cities throughout the nation. Warehouses were spread out to allow for faster shipping, getting product out in a timely manner to key markets. Due to the size and weight of LPs, which were still the dominant format, trucking companies did most of the shipping.

In October 1973, Syria and Egypt started a military conflict with Israel later called the Yom Kippur War. Although the war only lasted nineteen days, its impact was widespread. In retaliation for America's support of Israel, the Organization of Arab Petroleum Exporting Countries (OAPEC) reduced production and imposed an embargo on oil. The price of gasoline and heating oil rose precipitously in the years following the war. Petroleum is also a key ingedient in making vinyl records. The reduced availability during the embargo created increased manufacturing costs. The higher price of gasoline increased both shipping and manufacturing costs, cutting into profitability at the same time that retail sales were decreasing.

By the end of the decade, faced with increased expenses and declining sales, major labels needed to change their business practices to survive. Overseas conglomerates bought U.S. labels, shrinking the number of record companies and creating entertainment entities with cross-promotional opportunities in movies, concert tours, and television. Ironically, that was not unlike Al Bell's vision, which perhaps was both ahead of its time and underfunded. Regional offices were closed, including those in Memphis, leaving only New York, Nashville, and Los Angeles as centers of the record business. Warehouses closed and shipping was more efficiently managed.

Memphis was left as a city with a large creative population of musicians, producers, and engineers but no industry to support them.

★

With offices and staff consolidated into fewer markets, there were not as many opportunities for new artists. Tightened expenses resulted in fewer artist signings and lower production budgets. As a result, musicians who had played on hit records took non-music-related jobs to pay their bills.

Compact discs gained popularity in the 1980s and were seen as the savior of the declining record industry. Catalog sales, the source of cash flow and profitability for labels, increased as music lovers abandoned LPs and bought new copies of their libraries on CDs.

Launched in 1981, Music Television (MTV) had become a primary promotional tool by the end of the decade. Recording budgets changed to include music videos. With the now-critical influence of MTV and the added expense of filming videos, the major labels tightened their grip on making hit records.

Independent companies lacked the resources to compete for retail shelf space and access to MTV. Essentially, the record industry was split into a small number of multinational companies representing the majors and independent labels who were better suited to nurture and develop talent.

Although Memphis music had seen success and hit records, it historically depended on an independent spirit not bowed to commercial considerations. From the early bluesmen to jazz heroes, rock pioneers to soul shouters, the music typically was not the result of searching for a hit.

The bleak years of the late 1970s and early 1980s set the tone for everything that followed in the city's music.

★

The Orpheum Theatre has been on the corner of Beale and Main Streets since the 1920s. A former vaudeville house and movie theater, in 1976 it became a monopoly piece in downtown development.

As we entered the boardroom at City Hall in early October 1976, I could see I was the only one not wearing a suit. As the twenty-four-year-old music writer for the *City of Memphis* magazine, they forgave my attire, although I was clearly an outsider. The meeting was called to discuss the possibility of the City of Memphis buying the Orpheum Theatre from the local family who had operated it as a movie house for decades. The Jehovah's Witnesses had offered to purchase the property. Deadlines were set and passed. The owners were determined to sell that week to the church if the city refused.

That news rallied an interesting mix of people to the meeting. I was there with attorney Jack McNeil, a former city councilman and ardent music lover. Mayor J. Wyeth Chandler and his representatives attended along with several downtown developers, including Charlie Vergos, owner of the Rendezvous restaurant; businessman Al Sewell; and William M. Mathews Jr., the chairman of the board of Union Planters National Bank, the company that had just put Stax out of business.

The banker and developers planned a multimillion-dollar project for the block west of the theater overlooking the Mississippi River. I made an impassioned plea for the city to buy the building and convert it into a performing arts center. I recall the mayor saying, "That's all well and good, and I'm sure my wife would love that, but I can't spend taxpayer funds for that."[2]

That seemed to be the end of the conversation. In desperation, I turned to the developers and said something like, "Tomorrow, the building will be sold to the Jehovah's Witnesses. They are the pamphlet-giving group that knocks on your door hoping to save you. Do you guys want to put millions of dollars next door to them? I assure you they will find lots of lost souls in your place."[3]

The next day, the Orpheum was sold to the Memphis Development Foundation, a newly formed nonprofit made up of attendees from the meeting.

CHAPTER TWENTY-THREE

THE DAWN OF PUNK

"It was their music. It was something that Mama and Daddy hated."

—Sam Phillips, record producer

★

As the commercial music industry struggled in the late 1970s, Memphis found a new creative freedom unburdened by the need to be validated with hits. With top-notch studios and seasoned session musicians abandoned by the major companies, innovative recordings and live performances became the norm.

When the Memphis Development Foundation bought the Orpheum Theatre, they had no plans for it. The Orpheum was a 2,500-seat former vaudeville house that had fallen into disrepair. The appointed manager Hillsman Lee Wright was given a caretaker role and was open to anything that would bring people into the building while money was raised for a renovation.

For three weeks in 1978, the Orpheum hosted an event called the Tennessee Waltz, a spoof on The Last Waltz, the farewell performance of the influential group The Band. The event was billed as the retirement show of Mud Boy and the Neutrons, who nevertheless continued to play together until the murder of guitarist Lee Baker in 1996.

The Tennessee Waltz shows were an eclectic mix of talent featuring Furry Lewis with Lee Baker; Harmonica Frank Floyd; The Cramps, a New York–based punk rock band Alex Chilton was producing; an all-female band called The Klitz; and Mud Boy and the Neutrons. Noted Memphis photographer William Eggleston and his son crawled around stage filming the action with a video camera, a new invention at the time. I served as stage manager, which meant attempting to manage chaos and getting groups on and off the stage with equipment set up and ready.

During one of the breaks between bands, Gus Nelson, a transplanted Arkansan who had been filming blues artists around town, asked if he could play a song. He was a timid, quiet man who always seemed genuinely excited just to be around musicians. Wearing tattered tails and white gloves with the fingers cut off, Nelson came out from backstage carrying an electric guitar and a chain saw. He looked somewhat like a cross between Charlie Chaplin and Mickey Mouse. No one knew Gus played an instrument until he did an awkward version of Lead Belly's "The Bourgeois Blues" still in gloves and finally chain-sawing

Marcia Clifton and Amy Gassner of The Klitz relaxing with Panther Burns' vocalist Tav Falco, Memphis

the plugged-in guitar. The noise was horrific. Alex Chilton grinned widely. A star was born.

★

Gus Nelson was a funny kind of guy. He seemed to be around everywhere innovative music was presented, often with a video camera and always with a pleasant disposition. The son of Italian immigrants, he was transplanted from Philadelphia and must have felt out of place growing up in rural Arkansas.

When Gus finished playing "The Bourgeois Blues" and chain-sawed his instrument, Chilton knew what he wanted to do. The previous year, a British band called the Sex Pistols had introduced punk music to the United States, including a Memphis stop on their only tour.

Chilton had been experimenting with punk rock both with The Cramps, a New York–based group, and The Klitz, an all-female band who could barely play their instruments. In Nelson, he found the perfect foil for his ideas for a performance art rock band. He approached

The Klitz members Lesa Aldridge on guitar with Gail Clifton singing at the Orpheum Theatre, Memphis

Nelson about starting a band together that would feature Gus on guitar and vocals. Nelson's given name was Gustavo Falco; it was changed by his adoptive father. He became known as Tav Falco at Alex's suggestion. They added drummer Ross Johnson and a rotating cast of non-musicians on various instruments, including synthesizer and trumpet. The band was named Panther Burns after a town in Mississippi, where the residents were rumored to have trapped a black panther that had been killing livestock and burned it alive. The screams of the animal were said to be nerve-racking. Appropriately, Panther Burns' shows were often nerve-racking.

Chilton wanted to include musicians with non-musicians who had different artistic backgrounds in a setting with no commercial aspirations. The result was Nelson singing with abandon and playing guitar horribly out of tune. Drummer Ross Johnson kept the beat but usually followed the raw rhythm set down by Tav. All against the sound cloud of Eric Hill's synthesizer ramblings and Rick Ivy's trumpet bleats.

As the only accomplished musician in the group, Alex seemed to relish the undisciplined noise and unstructured chaos. I watched Falco tune his guitar before going onstage only to have Chilton reach over and indiscriminately turn the keys to untune it.

By the time Chilton left the band, Tav Falco had become a performer with his own following. He moved to Vienna, Austria, and continues to record and tour with a rotating cast of musicians. Alex Chilton made several innovative solo records reuniting with Jody Stephens for Big Star events and recording a live show and a studio album with Ken Stringfellow and Jon Auer, members of the band The Posies.

★

Panther Burns, The Klitz, and Jim Dickinson performed a series of shows in a downtown loft shortly after the Tennessee Waltz. The first loft show was February 10, 1979. They sometimes included older Memphis musicians Cordell Jackson and Charlie Feathers on the bill as a nod to the music's originators.

By 1979, with a following established at the lofts, a more permanent home for punk was needed. Tav Falco assumed the role of punk rock impresario when he found an outlet for the music. The Well was a dive, usually empty save for a few painters and craftsmen who stopped by for a beer after work. The front windows were painted black and graffiti covered the walls. Across from the door was a shuffleboard table, and a large bar took up much of the wall to the left. The floor was broken tile, chipped and dirty from years of spilled drinks and abuse. The low dropped ceiling was missing sections. Flickering fluorescent lights created an eerie funeral home effect. The smell of smoke from cigarettes and marijuana was sometimes overwhelmed by beer and vomit.

The owners were an older married couple who hated the music, the bands, and the audiences, but they liked the money generated by packed houses. Other bands joined The Klitz and Panther Burns to turn the venue into a nurturing ground for punk rock.

Shows billed for 10:00 p.m. often started after midnight. In addition to Panther Burns and The Klitz, groups like the Randy Band and Mud Boy and the Neutrons drew crowds of music lovers intrigued by the uncommercial sounds and stage antics. For a few years, The Well was home to the punk movement in Memphis. The owners finally tired of the crowds, selling the club to a couple of young entrepreneurs named James Barker and Phillip Stratton in 1981.

Barker and Stratton cleaned the floors, painted the walls black, and installed a series of televisions that played music videos. Changing the name to the Antenna Club, they began booking out-of-town bands. Much of the original crowd, who were attracted to the rawness of the venue, refused to come back. As punk became more established, its audience changed to include college and high school kids, and the venue eventually held shows that admitted all ages.

In a sense, the bands at The Well set the template for much of the city's music that followed. The freedom of producing art without commercial considerations allowed Memphis's independent spirit to thrive.

The same culture of innovation that drove Sam Phillips, Jim Stewart, Booker Little, and Jim Dickinson to creative peaks continues today. There have been commercial successes since the industry changed, but contemporary Memphis musicians are not driven by elusive record sales.

★

People like to talk about good music versus bad music. Often these qualifiers move along generational lines. Beginning with swing music and continuing through rap and hip-hop, older listeners seemed to denigrate the music of their children. And that's just how the kids want it. It empowers them to have opinions different than their parents and is often a first step in establishing a sense of independence and individuality.

In his interview with Peter Guralnick, Sam Philips said, "It was simply because I knew that young people . . . did not have their music. I mean, that is a very important thing. . . . So, can you blame a young person grabbing an eighty-nine-cent record or a seventy-nine-cent record and taking it home and wearing that damn thing out . . . it was their music. It was something that Mama and Daddy hated . . . it doesn't take a PhD in psychology to figure that out."[1]

I personally don't believe in the notion of bad music. Obviously, there are degrees of creativity, thematic nuance, and musicality, and these can play into the attractiveness of musical preferences. People have an emotional response and connection to music. The feelings are always valid. Are those feelings somehow less real for a preteen listening to a Disney pop song than for a classical music lover or a jazz aficionado?

If music touches your soul—regardless of age, demographics, or education—it serves its purpose. It connects you to the artist, to the songwriter, and often to your generation.

CHAPTER TWENTY-FOUR

MUSIC TOURISM: MEMPHIS CASHES IN

"To me, art is the rooster or the dog before the earthquake. It tells you what's going on down under there. It tells you what structural changes are getting ready to happen in your society."
—Sid Selvidge, musician

★

Elvis Presley was a generous man who never abandoned his hometown. He famously gave Cadillacs and expensive gifts to friends and strangers. A trauma center at a local hospital is named for him, and there has been a push for years to name Memphis's airport in his honor.

But Elvis's greatest gift to Memphis was the timing of his death. He died of an apparent heart attack on August 16, 1977, at his Graceland home. The date was far enough removed from the July 4 holiday but earlier than Labor Day when most schools started. Fans could visit the city without conflicts of school or other holiday activity.

★

I had contributed a few reviews to *Rolling Stone* magazine in the mid-1970s. When news of Presley's death was announced, I phoned my editor. I remember the conversation like this.

"Elvis just died," I said. "Do you want me to run out to Graceland and do a little piece on it?"

"Everyone's coming in," replied my editor. "Every flight and hotel room are booked up."

Growing up in Memphis, I assumed that my hometown was unremarkable. Every town must have local record labels with studios and some local version of Rufus Thomas on the radio. There must be an alternate Elvis, Isaac Hayes, Charlie Rich, and Jerry Lee Lewis in every city. By that hot August day in 1977, I had researched Memphis music enough to understand its worldwide impact. But I clearly didn't appreciate Elvis's stature.

After 100,000 people lined the streets outside of Graceland, everything in Memphis changed. Politicians and city leaders who had been embarrassed by Presley recognized the worldwide adulation for him. And they saw the potential for revenue.

By 1977, both Stax and Hi Records were no longer in town, but Elvis's death opened the door for a music tourism industry, which was worth $3.6 billion in 2019 and drew 12.4 million visitors. Open to tourists, Presley's home is the second most-visited private residence in the country, and the yearly "death day" celebration draws thousands of visitors from around the world.

Elvis's death was the impetus for the completion of the city-owned Beale Street entertainment district, which opened in 1982, the same year Graceland began tours. Museums opened to tell the story of Stax Records, Sun Records, blues, and the overall history of the city's music.

Elvis's Graceland home opened its doors to the public on June 7, 1982, and Sun Records started offering guided tours of its studio in 1987. The Stax Records studio on McLemore Avenue was razed in 1989, but a replica built on the same spot opened in May 2003. The Memphis Rock 'n' Soul Museum, created by the Smithsonian Institution, was the culmination of more than ten years' research. It welcomed visitors for the first time on April 29, 2000.

Music had been a force in the Memphis economy for decades, beginning with the commercial successes of Sun, Hi, and Stax Records. Just as the change in the record business created a void in traditional record company finances, music tourism grew to become a major source of revenue for a city in need of new industry. In a follow-up article marking the tenth anniversary of Elvis's death in *U.S. News & World Report*, Judy Peiser of the Center for Southern Folklore said, "Elvis died so we could pay our taxes."[1]

Memphis's tradition of great musicians fostered a prosperous tourism industry centered on the city's music history. An unfortunate side effect saw younger active artists competing for attention with legacy ones. Innovative players are still working every night in bars, clubs, and studios, often for little money or recognition.

Memphis has always been a tough town for musicians. The multibillion-dollar music tourism business has not changed that condition for contemporary acts. Today, musicians play for as little as fifty dollars per night. The music is alive and vibrant as ever, but the financial support has remained the same.

"The problem is that people think we are 'playing' music," said Larry Raspberry. "They don't recognize this is our work."[2]

★

As expected with its long history of black music, hip-hop and rap, which began as underground music in New York in the 1980s, thrive in contemporary Memphis. Three 6 Mafia, Yo Gotti, Al Kapone, and 8Ball & MJG are just a few of the artists in the burgeoning rap scene.

The tradition of music spanning generations continues. Jim Dickinson's children, Luther and Cody, perform together as the North Mississippi Allstars. James Alexander's son Phalon adopted the name Jazze Pha and is a successful producer. Sid Selvidge's son Steve is an in-demand studio guitarist and a member of several nationally prominent bands. Saxophonist Kirk Whalum, who grew up in a musical family, has a son named Kyle who is a bassist and a nephew, Kenneth Whalum III, who has recorded with Jay-Z, John Legend, and Joss Stone.

I have been asked from time to time to speak to young people interested in a career in music. My recommendation is always the same: "Don't do it unless you just can't be happy doing anything else." For speaking this truth, I am no longer asked to speak to young people about a career in music. What I was trying to convey was that music is not

DAVID LESS

ABOVE: Luther Dickinson and Jim Dickinson listen to playbacks at Zebra Ranch Studio, Coldwater, Mississippi

RIGHT: Sid Selvidge with Mudboy and the Neutrons at WEVL radio station concert, Memphis

RICK IVY

a career. It's a consuming passion. Elvis Presley, Rufus Thomas, Steve Cropper, Isaac Hayes, and scores of other Memphis artists began life in working-class families and chose music because the playing field was even. Race, social standing, and lack of education were not barriers to success in music.

They didn't expect fame and wealth, but music made them happy. During the halcyon years of the 1960s and 1970s, the local industry provided income for many writers, singers, and musicians and supported businesses. Today's musicians learn their craft for the love of music.

It's vital, real, and innovative. The industry changed in the 1980s, but the independent spirit of music remains a core part of the city's DNA. The music that was born in Memphis represents white and black artists reaching for each other and eventually finding common ground.

Sid Selvidge shared his views on this during my interview with him in 2000: "To me, art is the rooster or the dog before the earthquake. It tells you what's going on down under there. It tells you what structural changes are getting ready to happen in your society. I think that's basically what the coming together of the cultures into rock and roll and the continuation of the blues and the evolution of soul music. It allowed African Americans an avenue toward affluence and integration within a larger cultural context, into an American context rather than an ethnic context. I think you saw this first with the music."[3]

★

The most commercially successful Memphis-born artist of the twenty-first century started his career as a member of *The All New Mickey Mouse Club* in 1993. The original version of the Disney-produced television show began in 1955. Justin Timberlake left the show and in 1995 became a member of the popular singing group *NSYNC, then embarking on a vastly successful solo career in 2002.

Comparisons to Elvis Presley accelerated when Timberlake saw success with an acting career. Two of the most famous singers from Memphis had both ventured into a film career following tremendous success as a recording artist. Timberlake had won Grammys, Emmys, Billboard Music, American Music, People's Choice, and MTV Video awards by 2015. But his words at his 2015 induction into the Memphis Music Hall of Fame stand out. When Timberlake came onstage to accept the honor, he said, "I'm serious. This is the fucking coolest thing that's ever happened to me."[4]

EPILOGUE

"I wanted to meow like a cat, but I figured that was too hip."
—Fred Ford, musician

★

Memphis was obviously not the only place in America that suffered the effects of racism. The yellow fever epidemics in the 1870s created a racial anomaly between less mobile black Memphians and a white population that fled until the crisis ended. This lasted well into the twentieth century until the advent of mass media and more efficient transportation options reduced regionalism.

Unfortunately, racism in Memphis has not disappeared. While it was overt in the past, it grew subtler and probably no worse than other American cities. The 2016 election of President Donald Trump has emboldened racists and anti-Semitic people to bring these attitudes out of the shadows and into the light.

There have been moments of triumph where Memphis seemed to confront racism and turn its tide. Representative Harold Ford's election to Congress in 1974 against a white four-term Republican incumbent signaled a turning point in black political power. Ford is a son of funeral home owner N.J. Ford, an influential and respected member of Memphis's African American elite. With his election, Representative Ford forced

Memphis's power brokers and business community to work with him on an equal footing. It led to a political structure where blacks and whites needed each other to govern.

The transition to shared power continued with the historic election of W.W. Herenton to city mayor in 1991 by a slim margin of 172 votes. Like Ford, he defeated a white long-term incumbent, Richard Hackett. Mayor Herenton was reelected five times, eventually resigning in 2009 for an unsuccessful run for Congress.

★

In July 2015, white Memphis Police officer Connor Schilling shot and killed Darrius Stewart, a black teenager, during a routine traffic stop. This followed a similar shooting by white police officer Darren Wilson of black teenager Michael Brown on August 9, 2014, in Ferguson, Missouri. In both cases, a grand jury decided to not press charges against the police officers who shot the unarmed, uncharged, young black men. The outrage over these and other killings of African Americans by police spawned a national movement called Black Lives Matter.

July 2016 became a time of national racial unrest precipitated by two more killings of black men on the same day—July 6—by police in Baton Rouge, Louisiana, and St. Anthony, Minnesota. The next day during a Black Lives Matter protest in Dallas, Texas, Micah Johnson—who was not part of the demonstration—shot five police officers killing them and wounding nine others. Tensions were at a peak as Black Lives Matter demonstrations were held in cities across the nation.

In Memphis, a permit was issued, and an early evening march was planned for Sunday, July 10, 2016, from the Lorraine Motel, now the National Civil Rights Museum to the plaza in front of FedExForum, a multipurpose arena situated downtown near Beale Street.

The crowd that assembled at the plaza comprised nearly 200 marchers, including some who were affiliated with Memphis street gangs. Social media posts urged more people to gather, but not all of them were directly associated with the Black Lives Matter movement. The various agendas of those who had convened were somewhat in conflict, and tensions among the different groups ran high until alleged gang member

Frank Gottie, aka Frank Gibson, grabbed a bullhorn and led a march north on B.B. King Boulevard toward the Criminal Justice Center, the holding jail for detainees awaiting trial.

When Gottie and the protesters reached the Criminal Justice Center, they were met by a heavy police presence, so they continued the march to the Memphis-Arkansas Memorial Bridge. Thanks to social media posts, a large group joined them at the jail, the mixed-race crowd now numbered close to a thousand, comprising gang members, Black Lives Matters protesters, and young and old Memphians inspired by the moment.

Memphis is situated at the intersection of I-40, the nation's major east-west interstate, and I-55, a major north-south one. An average of 48,000 cars traverse I-40 over the Memphis-Arkansas Memorial Bridge daily.

Police tried to stop the marchers from going onto the bridge, but a group broke off from the front and entered through another ramp. By the time the officers could respond, the crowd had taken the bridge and shut down traffic. The standoff lasted hours. Several factors gave it the potential for a violent confrontation: the summer heat made both protesters and police, who were in riot gear, uncomfortable; several Black Lives Matter demonstrations held in other cities since the Dallas police murders had disintegrated into riots; and the makeup of the Memphis crowd included an uneasy mix of peaceful activists, gang members, college students, families, and Black Lives Matter protesters.

Mayor Jim Strickland, the first white mayor of Memphis in twenty-five years, had been sworn in only seven months previously. He had yet to appoint a permanent police director, instead naming Mike Rallings, a veteran African American deputy chief, as the interim head of the department.

Rallings headed to the bridge to try to negotiate with the protesters to open the bridge to traffic, which was now backed up for miles. In a seemingly impossible situation, caught between his own irritated officers and an increasingly vocal crowd, this native son of Memphis remarkably managed to end the standoff in a peaceful manner. His staff had insisted that he wear a Kevlar bulletproof vest to the bridge. Speaking to the crowd through a bullhorn, Rallings conspicuously removed the vest and walked arm-in-arm with the leaders of the protest off the bridge and back to FedExForum. The crowd followed as Memphians watched this broadcast live on television.

Black and white residents had joined in a show of solidarity, opposing violence against African Americans by authority figures. Rallings followed this victory by asking the community to refrain from murder for thirty days. Unfortunately, that request seemed impossible, the pause lasting only a few days.

★

Fred Ford was a giant of a man with broad shoulders, dark skin, and huge hands. He had white hair and a long white beard that made him look like a black Santa Claus. Fred can be heard howling like a dog at the end of Big Mama Thornton's "Hound Dog." He once told me, "I wanted to meow like a cat, but I figured that was too hip." He toured and played baritone saxophone with Johnny Otis's and Clarence "Gatemouth" Brown's bands. When he played and danced onstage, his persona was Sweet Daddy Goodloe.

Ford, who toured the world playing music, produced a Grammy-winning album with his old friend Phineas Newborn Jr. in 1974. He was cofounder of the Memphis in May Beale Street Music Festival in 1977, an annual three-day event drawing audiences of more than 100,000. His career spanned decades, and he exemplified many established traits of a Memphis musician: he came through the city high school bands; played with the great jazz players in the 1950s; recorded at the Hi, Ardent, and American Sound studios; and worked with many great Memphis musicians including Alex Chilton.

Despite his talent and accomplishments, he never received the deserved recognition in his hometown. When Fred was diagnosed with cancer, his financial situation was dire. Members of the music community felt that Ford should leave this world with an appropriate funeral, free of debt. If he somehow beat the disease, money would be available for his recovery.

He approved when I told him of our plan for a fundraiser called Fredstock. I secured the New Daisy Theatre on Beale Street as a donated

SMITHSONIAN INSTITUTION ARCHIVES, ACCESSION 11-009, IMAGE #92-5061 11A, PHOTO BY PETE DANIEL

The author and Fred Ford
clowning for the camera,
Memphis, May 1992

venue for October 7, 1999. Every performer approached agreed to play
for free. I invited Rufus and Carla Thomas, Lucero, Charlie Wood, and
Emerson Able. Lucero later became a headlining act capable of selling
out larger venues while Charlie Wood found success as a jazz artist in
England. Both were beginning their careers in 1999 and were unable to
generate significant ticket sales. Concerned about the marquee for the
show, I called Alex Chilton who was living in New Orleans. Alex had
hired Fred for several of his records.

After I told Chilton about Ford's health and what we hoped to
accomplish with the fundraiser, I said, "I don't think I have a sellout
show. I need you to come in and we'll get you a band, so we can raise
more money for him."

"I'm sorry to hear about Fred, but there are no musicians in Memphis
I can play with," responded Alex.

Feeling my back against the wall, I replied. "How about the Hi
Rhythm Section?"

"That will work."[1]

With Alex Chilton and the Hi Rhythm Section included, the event was successful in raising enough money to settle Ford's medical bills and funeral.

★

I visited Fred often in the hospital and witnessed his decline. The last time I saw him was on November 26, 1999. He no longer looked like the giant that I knew. Small and frail, he could barely speak, his voice decimated from the throat cancer.

When I told Fred that the fundraiser had successfully raised enough money to settle his bills, he seemed gratified.

"I love you," he croaked.

I told him I loved him, too.

He died that day. The funeral procession was long, and remarkably, the sheriff's office assigned deputies to lead it. I watched amazed as the motorcycle officers closed the on-ramps to I-240 for the procession, something usually only done for politicians and dignitaries.

That day, Memphis finally got it right.

CHRONOLOGY OF SIGNIFICANT EVENTS IN MEMPHIS MUSIC

1800   First camp meeting is held in Logan County, Kentucky, in July.

1819   City of Memphis is founded on May 22.

1826   City of Memphis is incorporated on December 19 with a population of 500.

1865   U.S. Congress ratifies the Thirteenth Amendment on December 6, abolishing slavery.

1866   U.S. Congress ratifies the Fourteenth Amendment on July 9, guaranteeing citizenship and equal protection under the law regardless of race.

1870   U.S. Congress ratifies the Fifteenth Amendment on February 3, giving black males the right to vote.

1873   First of three yellow fever epidemics in Memphis begins.

1878   Third and worst of the yellow fever epidemics begins on August 5.

1879   The City of Memphis loses its charter.

1892   Three grocers are lynched on March 8, following the so-called Riot at the Curve.

1893   The charter for the City of Memphis is restored.

1907   Charles Harrison Mason starts the Church of God in Christ (COGIC) in Memphis.

1908   Wild Bill Latura kills six at Hammitt Ashford's saloon on Beale Street on December 10.

1909   W.C. Handy composes "The Memphis Blues" as a campaign song for Edward Hull Crump's mayoral run.

1912   W.C. Handy publishes "The Memphis Blues."

1917   W.C. Handy publishes "Beale Street Blues."

1927   RCA talent scout Ralph Peer comes to Memphis to record local blues artists and on February 24 records the Memphis Jug Band.

Jimmie Lunceford is hired at Manassas High School and begins a band program. Dub Jenkins starts his student band at Booker T. Washington High School.

1940   William Theodore McDaniel is hired as band director at Booker T. Washington High School.

Edward Hull "Boss" Crump orders Joe Boyle to clean up crime on Beale Street.

1941   William Theodore McDaniel becomes the band director at Manassas High School and continues at Booker T. Washington High School.

1942   The Plantation Inn opens in West Memphis, Arkansas.

1943   Mitchell's Hotel and Lounge opens on Beale Street. The lounge's name changes to Club Handy a few years later.

1945   Sam and Becky Phillips move to Memphis. Sam begins working for WREC radio.

1946   John Novarese and Joe Cuoghi buy Shirley's Poplar Tunes Record Shop on July 12.

1949   WDIA radio becomes the first station to feature black DJs playing music for a black audience.

Robert "Buster" Williams opens Plastic Products record-pressing plant.

Dewey Phillips debuts on-air at WHBQ radio.

1950   Sam Phillips opens Memphis Recording Service on January 3 at 706 Union Avenue.

Leonard "Doughbelly" Campbell is killed in a car crash in February.

1952   Sun Records is founded by Sam Phillips on March 27.

1954   *Brown v. Board of Education of Topeka* is settled by the U.S. Supreme Court on May 17, ruling that racial segregation in public education is unconstitutional.

Sam Phillips records Elvis Presley's "That's All Right" on July 5.

1955   All-female radio station WHER begins broadcasting on October 29 owned by Sam Phillips with financing by Kemmons Wilson.

Sam Phillips sells Elvis Presley's contract to RCA Records in November.

1956   Elvis Presley's "Heartbreak Hotel" is released in the United States on January 27. Shortly afterward, it is played on Radio Luxembourg, introducing him to European audiences.

WHBQ television launches *Phillips and His Phriends* hosted by Dewey Phillips on August 25.

Elvis Presley makes his first appearance on *The Ed Sullivan Show* on September 9.

WHBQ television gives Dewey Phillips a new afternoon show called *Pop Shop* beginning December 31.

1957   Hi Records is started by Joe Cuoghi and his partners.

Satellite Records is formed by siblings Jim Stewart and Estelle Axton in Brunswick, Tennessee.

1958   *American Bandstand* replaces Dewey Phillips's afternoon television show *Pop Shop*. Phillips moves to 11:30 p.m. time slot with a new show, *Night Beat*, on January 9, which is canceled after three days.

1959   Jerry Blankenship murders Carol Feathers on February 19, causing Danny's Club in West Memphis, Arkansas, to close.

1960   Sam Phillips opens his new studio at 639 Madison Avenue with a grand opening on September 17.

Poplar Tunes moves into their new building at 308 Poplar Avenue.

Chips Moman and Jim Stewart rent the Capitol Theatre and convert it into Satellite's studio.

Carla Thomas's duet with her dad, Rufus, is released on Satellite Records.

Leroy Hodges is hired for his first session with Willie Mitchell at Royal Studios.

Atlantic Records agrees to a distribution arrangement with Satellite Records.

1961   Memphis City Schools begin a restricted integration policy.

Booker Little dies on October 5 at age twenty-three from uremic poisoning.

The Mar-Keys "Last Night" is released on Satellite Records.

Satellite Records and studio change their name to Stax.

1962   "Green Onions" is released on Stax Records. Booker T. & the M.G.s is formed and becomes the house rhythm section.

Chips Moman quits Stax Records over a dispute about payments and ownership.

Otis Redding is signed to Stax Records.

1964   George Klein's *Talent Party* begins airing on WHBQ television.

Chips Moman opens American Sound Studio.

Andrew "Sunbeam" Mitchell opens Club Paradise.

The Bitter Lemon coffee shop opens.

Mabon "Teenie" Hodges joins Willie Mitchell's band.

1965   Donald "Duck" Dunn replaces Lewie Steinberg in Booker T. & the M.G.s, which now includes two white and two black members.

Leroy and Charles Hodges join their brother, Teenie, in Willie Mitchell's band.

1966   First Memphis Country Blues Festival is presented at the Overton Park Shell.

Memphis City Schools staff and students are fully integrated.

John Fry opens Ardent Studios at 1457 National Street.

1967   Reggie Young and Bobby Emmons quit Hi Records and join with Chips Moman to anchor the American Sound Studio's rhythm section.

Stax/Volt Revue tours Europe from March 17 through April 9.

Otis Redding and the Bar-Kays die in an airplane crash on December 10.

Dan Penn produces "The Letter" at American Sound Studio, featuring Alex Chilton and his band The Box Tops.

1968   Stax Records is sold to Gulf & Western.

The Reverend Dr. Martin Luther King Jr. is assassinated on April 4.

1969   Sam Phillips sells the Sun Records catalog to Nashville producer Shelby Singleton.

Ann Peebles signs with Hi Records.

Willie Mitchell's band is in a car accident on the way to Atchison, Kansas.

1970   Willie Mitchell signs Al Green to Hi Records.

Joe Cuoghi dies on July 13.

Ray Harris sells his shares in Hi Records to Willie Mitchell who becomes the label's vice president. Nick Pesce replaces Harris as president.

Jim Stewart and Al Bell buy Stax Records back from Gulf & Western.

1971   John Fry opens a new Ardent studio at 2000 Madison Avenue.

1972   Big Star's #1 Record is released on Ardent records, distributed by Stax Records.

Isaac Hayes wins the Academy Award on April 10 for the "Theme from *Shaft*."

Al Bell buys Jim Stewart's shares of Stax Records, becoming its sole owner. He signs a distribution agreement with Clive Davis at CBS Records.

Chips Moman closes the American Sound Studio and moves to Atlanta with most of the rhythm section.

Wattstax concert is presented and filmed in Los Angeles on August 20.

1973   Following U.S. District Judge Robert McRae Jr.'s April 20, 1972, order, Memphis City Schools begins a program of busing students in 1973, thus ending neighborhood schools.

Egypt and Syria attack Israel, beginning the Yom Kippur War on October 6.

OAPEC imposes oil embargo against the United States.

1974   Mary Woodson dies by suicide at the home of singer Al Green after scalding him in the bathtub on October 18.

Harold Ford is elected to U.S. Congress.

1975   Stax Records is forced into involuntary bankruptcy on December 19.

1976   Federal Bankruptcy Judge William Leffler orders Stax Records closed on January 12.

Malco Theatre Company sells the Orpheum Theatre to non-profit Memphis Development Foundation on October 7.

Al Jackson Jr. is murdered at his home on October 15.

Stax's publishing company (East Memphis Publishing) is sold.

Al Green founds the Full Gospel Tabernacle Church.

1977   Stax Records catalog is sold to Fantasy Records.

Hi Records is sold to Los Angeles–based Cream Records.

Elvis Presley dies on August 16 at his Graceland home.

1978   The Epstein cousins are murdered at Nathan and Sonny's Loan Company on October 6.

Three Tennessee Waltz concerts are produced at the Orpheum Theatre. Gus Nelson chainsaws his guitar while performing "Bourgeois Blues."

1979   Panther Burns' first show is presented on February 10 in a downtown loft at 96 South Front Street.

1981   Music Television (MTV) launches on August 1.

1991   Dr. W.W. Herenton becomes Memphis's first elected African American mayor on October 3.

1995   Justin Timberlake becomes a member of *NSYNC.

1996   Lee Baker dies on September 10.

2003   Sam Phillips dies on July 30.

2006   Three 6 Mafia win an Academy Award for "It's Hard Out Here for a Pimp."

2009   Jim Dickinson dies on August 15.

        Poplar Tunes record shop closes all stores in September.

2010   Alex Chilton dies on March 17.

2013   Sid Selvidge dies on May 2.

2015   Justin Timberlake is inducted into the Memphis Music Hall of Fame on October 17.

ACKNOWLEDGMENTS

This book has its origins in the mid-1970s when I moved back to Memphis from New York. Many of these ideas were formed during long conversations into the dead of night with Jim Dickinson, Memphis music griot, and Robert Palmer, a friend and mentor. Bob was a brilliant writer that was generous with his time and expertise to a young music lover. Jim's epitaph "I'm Not Gone. I'm Just Dead" rings as true today as when he died. Thanks to Augusta Palmer and Mary Lindsay Dickinson for keeping their flames alive.

Peter Guralnick and Anna Olswanger believed there was a book inside of me despite all evidence to the contrary. Their patience and encouragement helped me also believe it. Michael Holmes, Scott Isler, Howard Mandel, Crissy Calhoun, Shannon Parr, and Joan Guirdanella all improved the manuscript along the way with their comments and editing. Thanks to Jessica Albert, Susannah Ames, Emily Ferko, Aymen Saidane, and David Caron at ECW for their work on the finished product. Special thank you to Rick Ivy, Pete Daniel, Carleen Dorian Palmer, Erica Duncan, and Terry Manning for your photographs. Carol Givens, Mary Ann Aquadro, and Mary Ann Aquadro Linder for the use of certain images used in the book.

Stanley Booth, Duck Dunn, John Fry, Onzie Horne, Lee Baker, Jimmy Crosthwait and Sid Selvidge for their friendship over many years.

Thanks to Steve Selvidge, Boo Mitchell, Cody Dickinson, and Luther Dickinson for carrying on the tradition.

Fred Ford, Phineas Newborn Jr., and Furry Lewis for showing me how to live a life in music. Fred taught me about the contemporary realities of race and the transcendent power of music. Thomas Pinkston for his wisdom and the time he spent teaching me about racial history. Fred Hutchins for saving so much history. Bob Talley and Wilbur Steinberg, Memphis's Sunshine Boys, who were patient with me when I asked a million questions about Memphis music. Literally sitting at his feet during his home lectures, Professor John Quincy Wolfe's explanations of the beauty of indigenous art began my journey into the power of regional music.

Jerry Wexler, Willie Mitchell, and Ruth Brown for taking time to teach me about life and music. Rufus, Marvell, Vaneese, and Carla Thomas, the royal family of Memphis music. Teenie, Charles, and Leroy Hodges, Al Jackson, Howard Grimes, Alex Chilton, Floyd Newman, Don Bryant and Ann Peebles, Steve Cropper, Booker T. Jones, Don Nix, Isaac Hayes, Bobby Manual, Wayne Jackson, Andrew Love, and Onzie Horne Jr. all contributed to the soundtrack of the city. The world would be different without them.

Sam Phillips for changing the world. I will always value the friendship and kindness he and his family showed me and mine. Thanks to Knox and Jerry, Halley and the entire Phillips family (Skip, Johnny, Jud and Rose). Harmonica Frank Floyd, Billy Lee Riley, Sonny Burgess, Little Milton Campbell, Stan Kesler, and Roland Janes are friends that were branches of that tree.

Major Dowell, the last Zen master in the state of Mississippi, Dale Wilson, Varner Wilson, and Joe Smith, taught me how to work hard. Joe Orr, Erica Duncan, Dennis Smith, Andy Polk, and Rick Ivy for your friendship over the years.

John Novarese, Linda Alter, Frank Berretta, and Jimmy Burge who taught me the intricacies of the record industry.

I was fortunate enough to know, work, and learn from John Tigrett and Sidney Shlenker. I miss them both.

Martha Ellen Maxwell came to understand that on every major river in America, cities set off fireworks to the *1812 Overture* but there was only one Furry Lewis. That realization changed her life and contributed to her support of Memphis music and musicians.

Jim Dickinson, John Snyder, and Posey Hedges taught me how to produce a record. Sam Shoup, the most versatile musician in Memphis (or anywhere else), helped when I had specific questions during the writing of this book.

Bob Merlis for agreeing to go on the adventure of starting a record company with the idea of "putting the music back in the music business." Greg Geller, Martin Hawkins, Colin Escott, TV Tom Vickers, Billy F Gibbons, Jonathan Gould, Robert Gordon, and Pete Daniel, the collective brain trust of America's music.

Anise and Ron Belz, Rachel, and Rebecca. A lifetime of love and friendship has helped me countless times, especially when Ron told me it was time to get back to work after closing *Music Vision*.

Jody Stephens, Mark Jordan, Pat Mitchell Worley, and Elizabeth Montgomery Brown who have to suffer through my stories at lunch each Friday.

And finally, for my parents who always let me know that no matter how badly I screwed up, I would never be without a home.

NOTES

Interviews conducted for either the National Endowment for the Humanities (NEH) or Smithsonian Institution (SI) are designated as such in these endnotes. If a specific quote came from an interview section conducted by another member of the Smithsonian Institution research team, it also has the SI designation.

INTRODUCTION

1. David Less, "Raspberry Jam," *City of Memphis* magazine, December 1976, p. 46.
2. Steve Cropper, interview by the author, Nashville, Tennessee, December 10, 1999 (SI).
3. Marvell Thomas, interview by the author, Memphis, Tennessee, November 11, 1999 (SI).

CHAPTER ONE

1. Wayne Jackson, interview by the author, Memphis, Tennessee, November 9, 1999 (SI).
2. Andrew Love, interview by the author, Memphis, Tennessee, November 9, 1999 (SI).
3. Carla Thomas, interview by the author, Memphis, Tennessee, November 10, 1999 (SI).

4. Ann Peebles, interview by the author, Memphis, Tennessee, November 10, 1999 (SI).
5. Ibid.

CHAPTER TWO

1. Fred L. Hutchins, *What Happened in Memphis.* Kingsport, TN: Kingsport Press, Inc., 1965, pages 36–39.
2. Hutchins, page 38.
3. Hutchins, pages 39–40.

CHAPTER THREE

1. James Alexander, interview by the author, Memphis, Tennessee, April 1, 2000 (SI).
2. Ibid.
3. Dub Jenkins, interview by the author, New York, New York, March 10, 1979.
4. Emerson Able, interview by the author, Memphis, Tennessee, December 6, 1999 (SI).
5. William Ellis, "Professor W.T. McDaniel," Memphis Music Hall of Fame. Retrieved from memphismusichalloffame.com/inductee/profwtmcdaniel.
6. Floyd Newman, interview by the author, Memphis, Tennessee, February 23, 1998.
7. Andrew Love, interview by the author, Memphis, Tennessee, March 5, 1998.
8. John Branston, "City Beat," *Memphis Flyer*, May 19, 2004. Retrieved from memphisflyer.com/memphis/city-beat/Content?oid=1120879.

CHAPTER FOUR

1. Colin Escott and Martin Hawkins, *Catalyst: The Sun Records Story.* London: Aquarius Books, 1975, page 7.
2. Steve Cropper, interview by the author, Nashville, Tennessee, December 10, 1999 (SI).
3. Don Nix, interview by the author, Mount Pleasant, Tennessee, December 9, 1999 (SI).

4. Steve Cropper, interview by the author, Nashville, Tennessee, December 10, 1999 (SI).
5. Ibid.

CHAPTER FIVE

1. Don Nix, interview by the author, Mount Pleasant, Tennessee, December 9, 1999 (SI).
2. Ibid.
3. Steve Cropper, interview by the author, Nashville, Tennessee, December 10, 1999 (SI).
4. Charles Edmundson, "Slayer's Wife Recognizes Photograph of His Victim," *Commercial Appeal* (Memphis), February 21, 1960, section I, page 14.
5. Richard Connelly, "Drinking, Blind Anger Leads to Savage Bludgeon Slaying," *Commercial Appeal* (Memphis), February 21, 1960, section I, page 1.
6. Jim Dickinson, interview by Charles McGovern, Hernando, Mississippi, August 4, 1992 (SI).
7. Don Nix, interview by the author, Mount Pleasant, Tennessee, December 9, 1999 (SI).
8. Floyd Newman, interview by the author, Memphis, Tennessee, February 23, 1998.
9. Steve Cropper, interview by the author, Nashville, Tennessee, December 10, 1999 (SI).

CHAPTER SIX

1. *The Ed Sullivan Show*, CBS network, February 23, 1964.
2. John Lennon, interview by Marshall McLuhan, Canadian Broadcast Corporation, Toronto, Ontario, December 19, 1969.
3. Hunter Davies, *The Beatles: The Authorized Biography*. New York: McGraw Hill, 1968, page 19.
4. Keith Richards, *Life*. Boston: Back Bay Books, 2010, page 38.
5. Richards, page 87.
6. Email from Jonathan Gould to the author, April 5, 2019.
7. Al Green, interview by the author, Memphis, Tennessee, December 15, 1978.

8. Steve Cropper, interview by the author, Nashville, Tennessee, December 10, 1999 (SI).
9. Willie Mitchell, interview by the author, Memphis, Tennessee, August 1, 1979.
10. Colin Escott and Martin Hawkins, *Catalyst: The Sun Records Story*. London: Aquarius Books, 1975, page 7.

CHAPTER SEVEN

1. Jim Dickinson, interview by Pete Daniel, Hernando, Mississippi, August 4, 1992 (SI).
2. Don Nix, interview by the author, Mount Pleasant, Tennessee, December 9, 1999 (SI).
3. Sid Selvidge, interview by the author, Memphis, Tennessee, November 17, 2000.
4. Sid Selvidge, interview by the author, Memphis, Tennessee, November 17, 2000.
5. Billy Gibbons, interview by Chris Davis, Stephen Deusner, Chris Herrington and Andrew Earles, "On Top," *Memphis Flyer*, May 2, 2013.
6. Sid Selvidge, interview by the author, Memphis, Tennessee, November 17, 2000.
7. Ibid.

CHAPTER EIGHT

1. Walter "Furry" Lewis, interview by Carleen Dorian and the author, Memphis, Tennessee, August 7, 1977.
2. Fred Hutchins, interview by the author, Memphis, Tennessee, December 27, 1978.
3. Fred Hutchins, *What Happened in Memphis*. Kingsport, TN: Kingsport Press, 1965, page 47.
4. Quoted from Memphis author Devin Greaney who sourced the News Scimitar newspaper. In an email Greaney believed it to date from August 1912.
5. David Cohn, *Where I Was Born and Raised*. Notre Dame, IN: University of Notre Dame Press, 1967. Retrieved from users.soc. umn/edu/~samaha/cases/cohn_delta.html.

6. John "Peter" Chatman, aka Memphis Slim, interview by the author, Memphis, Tennessee, September 27, 1978 (NEH).

7. Maurice Hulbert, interview by the author, Memphis, Tennessee, June 27, 1979 (NEH).

8. Ibid.

9. Ibid.

10. Ibid.

11. Thomas Pinkston, interview by the author, Memphis, Tennessee, December 19, 1978 (NEH).

CHAPTER NINE

1. Thomas Pinkston, interview by the author, Memphis, Tennessee, December 19, 1978 (NEH).

2. Andrew Chaplin, interview by the author, Memphis, Tennessee, February 9, 1993.

3. Miles Davis, Quincy Troupe, and Jure Potokar, *Miles: The Autobiography*. New York: Simon and Schuster Paperbacks, 1989, page 262.

4. Leonard Feather, liner notes to *The Great Jazz Piano of Phineas Newborn Jr.*, Phineas Newborn Jr., Contemporary Records, M3611, LP, 1961.

5. Leonard Feather, liner notes to *Please Send Me Someone to Love*, Phineas Newborn Jr., Contemporary Records, S7622, LP, 1969.

6. Andrew "Sunbeam" Mitchell, interview by the author, Memphis, Tennessee, June 26, 1979.

7. Ibid.

8. Willie Mitchell, interview by the author, Memphis, Tennessee, August 1, 1979.

9. Fred Ford, interview by the author, Memphis, Tennessee, May 20, 1992.

10. Emerson Able, interview by the author, Memphis, Tennessee, December 6, 1999 (SI).

CHAPTER TEN

1. Robert Levin, "Introducing Booker Little," *All About Jazz*. July 25, 2010. Retrieved from allaboutjazz.com/introducing-booker-little-booker-little-by-robert-levin.php.

2. Liner notes to *Out Front*, Booker Little Jr., Candid Records, 8027, LP, 1961.

3. Willie Mitchell, interview by the author, Memphis, Tennessee, August 1, 1979.

4. Joop Visser, liner notes to *Dexter Gordon Settin' the Pace*, Dexter Gordon, Proper Records, PROPERBOX 16, CD, 2001.

5. Fred Ford, interview by the author, Memphis, Tennessee, May 20, 1992.

6. Ibid.

7. Aleksandr Solzhenitsyn, *Cancer Ward*, New York: Vintage Books, 1968, page 272.

CHAPTER ELEVEN

1. Gilbert Chase, *America's Music*. New York: McGraw Hill Book Company, 1955, pages 207–209, 230.

2. "Jerry Lee Lewis & Sam Phillips - Religious Discussion (1957)," video posted to YouTube by Robin Haugsnes, published January 23, 2009. Retrieved from youtu.be/N-wsEcmwJKo.

3. Bill Ellis, "Lucie Campbell," Memphis Music Hall of Fame. Retrieved from memphismusichalloffame.com/inductee/luciecampbell.

4. Robert M. Marovich, *A City Called Heaven: Chicago and the Birth of Gospel Music*. Champaign, IL: University of Illinois Press, 2015, pages 27–47.

5. Robert Gordon, *Memphis Rent Party*. New York: Bloomsbury Publishing, 2018, page 149.

CHAPTER TWELVE

1. Rosie Gray, "Trump Defends White-Nationalist Protesters: 'Some Very Fine People on Both Sides'." *The Atlantic*, August 15, 2017. Retrieved from theatlantic.com/politics/archive/2017/08/trump-defends-white-nationalist-protesters-some-very-fine-people-on-both-sides/537012.

2. Jerry Wexler, interview by the author, Muscle Shoals, Alabama, June 14, 1980.

3. Nate Evans, interview by the author, Memphis, Tennessee, May 7, 1979.

4. Thomas Pinkston, interview by the author, Memphis, Tennessee, December 19, 1978.
5. Nate Evans, interview by the author, Memphis, Tennessee, May 7, 1979.
6. Thomas Pinkston, interview by the author, Memphis, Tennessee, December 19, 1978.

CHAPTER THIRTEEN

1. Author's private conversation with Jack Clement, Nashville, Tennessee, December 10, 1999.
2. Sam Phillips, interview by Peter Guralnick, Memphis, Tennessee, May 22, 1992 (SI).
3. Roland Janes, interview by the author, Memphis, Tennessee, January 27, 1998 (SI).
4. Ibid.
5. Sam Phillips, interview by Peter Guralnick, Memphis, Tennessee, May 22, 1992 (SI).
6. Paul Burlison, interview by the author, Horn Lake, Mississippi, January 20, 1998.

CHAPTER FOURTEEN

1. Jerry Wexler, interview by the author, Muscle Shoals, Alabama, June 13, 1980.
2. Ibid.
3. Rufus Thomas, interview by Pete Daniel, Memphis, Tennessee, August 5, 1992 (SI).
4. Betty Berger, interview by Charlie McGovern, Memphis, Tennessee, August 4, 1992 (SI).
5. Becky Phillips, interview by the author, Memphis, Tennessee, December 3, 1999 (SI).
6. Ibid.
7. Louis Cantor, *Dewey and Elvis*. Champaign, Illinois: University of Illinois Press, 2005, page 177–178.
8. George Klein, interview by the author, Memphis, Tennessee, February 4, 1998.

CHAPTER FIFTEEN

1. John Novarese, interview by the author, Memphis, Tennessee, August 10, 1992 (SI).
2. Ibid.
3. Bill Dries, "Marking History," *Memphis Daily News*, August 22, 2012. Retrieved from memphisdailynews.com/news/2012/aug/22/marking-history.
4. John Novarese, interview by the author, Memphis, Tennessee, August 10, 1992 (SI).
5. Ibid.
6. Ibid.

CHAPTER SIXTEEN

1. Email exchange with Martin Hawkins, Colin Escott, and Peter Guralnick, October 17, 2018.
2. Reggie Young, interview by the author, Franklin, Tennessee, January 19, 1998.
3. Ibid.
4. John Novarese, interview by the author, Memphis, Tennessee, August 10, 1992 (SI).
5. Reggie Young, interview by the author, Franklin, Tennessee, January 19, 1998.

CHAPTER SEVENTEEN

1. Charles Hodges, interview by the author, Memphis, Tennessee, July 15, 2019.
2. Mabon "Teenie" Hodges, interview by the author, Memphis, Tennessee, April 2, 2000 (SI).
3. Charles Hodges, interview by Pete Daniel, Memphis, Tennessee, December 7, 1999 (SI).
4. Author's private conversation with Jim Dickinson.
5. Jim Stewart, interview by the author, Memphis, Tennessee, May 19, 1992 (SI).
6. Willie Mitchell, interview by the author, Memphis, Tennessee, August 1, 1979.

CHAPTER EIGHTEEN

1. Wayne Jackson, interview by the author, Memphis, Tennessee, November 9, 1999 (SI).
2. Steve Cropper, interview by the author, Nashville, Tennessee, December 10, 1999 (SI).
3. Jim Stewart, interview by the author, Memphis, Tennessee, May 19, 1992 (SI).
4. Steve Cropper, interview by the author, Nashville, Tennessee, December 10, 1999 (SI).
5. Ibid.
6. Robert "Honeymoon" Garner, interview by the author, Memphis, Tennessee, December 6, 1999 (SI).

CHAPTER NINETEEN

1. Jonathan Gould, *Otis Redding: An Unfinished Life*. New York: Crown Archetype, 2017, page 13.
2. Donald "Duck" Dunn, interview by the author, Tunica, Mississippi, February 26, 1998.
3. Ben Cauley, interview by the author, Memphis, Tennessee, December 4, 1999 (SI).
4. James Alexander, interview by the author, Memphis, Tennessee, April 1, 2000 (SI).
5. Deanie Parker, interview by the author, Memphis, Tennessee, November 7, 1999 (SI).
6. Ibid.

CHAPTER TWENTY

1. Reggie Young, interview by the author, Franklin, Tennessee, January 19, 1998.
2. Dan Penn, interview by the author, Memphis, Tennessee, April 6, 2000.
3. Reggie Young, interview by the author, Franklin, Tennessee, January 19, 1998.
4. Ibid.
5. John Fry, interview by the author, Memphis, Tennessee, November 8, 1999 (SI).

6. Ibid.
7. Ibid.
8. Ibid.
9. Ibid.

CHAPTER TWENTY-ONE

1. Al Green, interview by the author, Memphis, Tennessee, December 15, 1978.
2. Ibid.
3. Howard Grimes, interview by the author, Memphis, Tennessee, November 12, 1999 (SI).
4. Ibid.

CHAPTER TWENTY-TWO

1. "U.S. Recorded Music Revenues by Format, 1973 to 2019," Recording Industry Association of America® (RIAA). Retrieved from riaa.com/u-s-sales-database.
2. Author's recollection of the meeting. October, 1976, Memphis City Hall conference room.
3. Ibid.

CHAPTER TWENTY-THREE

1. Sam Phillips, interview by Peter Guralnick, Memphis, Tennessee, May 22, 1992 (SI).

CHAPTER TWENTY-FOUR

1. Joseph P. Shapiro, "The King is dead, but his rich legacy still grows," *U.S. News & World Report*, August 24, 1987, page 56.
2. Author's private conversation with Larry Raspberry, 1976.
3. Sid Selvidge, interview by the author, Memphis, Tennessee, November 17, 2000.
4. Memphis Music Hall of Fame Induction Ceremony, Memphis, Tennessee, October 14, 2015. Retrieved from https://www.rollingstone.com/music/music-news/watch-justin-timberlakes-memphis-music-hall-of-fame-induction-ceremony-191022

EPILOGUE

1. Telephone conversation with Alex Chilton, September 1999.

Get the
eBook free!*

*proof of purchase
required

At ECW Press, we want you to enjoy this book in whatever format you like, whenever you like. Leave your print book at home and take the eBook to go! Purchase the print edition and receive the eBook free. Just send an email to ebook@ecwpress.com and include:

- the book title
- the name of the store where you purchased it
- your receipt number
- your preference of file type: PDF or ePub

A real person will respond to your email with your eBook attached. And thanks for supporting an independently owned Canadian publisher with your purchase!